Blueprint for 100 Deals or More Than $1 Million Per Year in Income

The exact systems and technology to
sell 100+ homes, every year ~
no matter the market

By

Alan Shafran and Rick Bengson

Authors: Alan Shafran and Rick Bengson
Cover Design: Michael Funk-Rokei
Editor: Katy Dean Cebe

ISBN: 0615474357
ISBN - 13: 9780615474359

"If you have a desire to build a big business in the real estate industry, Alan is revealing his step by step guide on how to do it."
- Tom Ferry
"North America's Top Real Estate Coach"

"Alan has been one of our company's top brokers in Southern California for years, producing millions of dollars in volume through the incredible use of networking, relationship building, technology, systems and a relentless discipline around training. Any sales professional striving to reach the next level should read this book... and if needed read it more than once!"

- Mark Johnson
Vice President Marketing and Sales Technology
Prudential California Realty a HomeServices of America
and Berkshire Hathaway Affiliate

Table of Contents

Preface

100 vs. 1

You probably bought this book because you want to know, *"How can I sell one hundred homes per year every single year?"* The answer follows the same equation for anyone entering the real estate business and it's better posed as: *would you rather be an individual agent, going it alone, or be part of a team?*

One is the loneliest number. This simple correlation is key throughout our **Blueprint for 100 Deals** – the systems, tools, and technologies of us, the authors of this book, Alan Shafran and Rick Bengson.

Whether you're a complete novice to the industry or you're a REALTOR® looking to ascend the ladder, our 100 Deals system and the expertise behind it can help you build your business, as well as make more money, please more customers, and improve your overall quality of life!

Based on a team building philosophy, this book will change the way you think about being a team player, your role in an existing team or the value of being part of a team. In addition, we explore the role of an effective team leader, how to get better results from your team members, and how to excel in your goal of reaching 100 deals a year, no matter the market conditions.

How? The first step is checking your ego at the door. Your family probably wants it checked, your spouse definitely wants it checked, and in your business, you cannot let it blind you from becoming successful. It's time to get real about real estate, and that means focusing on building a team, making a million dollars a year by doing 100 deals, utilizing the technology available so you can succeed, and still having a life. One typically cannot do 100 deals year after year without building a functional team – not a dysfunctional team, but a functional one; a team with a leader and team members who know and perform their roles. Think of how exciting this will be if you come from a dysfunctional family team and now, by following a book, you can be part of a functional family team. Because as teams become successful and the work is enjoyed, it soon becomes a second family.

Early in our careers, we realized that without balancing work and home life, the rewards are gained at the expense of one over the other. Unless you can establish a functional team environment – one that supports you, fosters a solid working relationship with your team-mates, and gives your clients the speedy and reliable service they deserve – you'll be carrying the burden of everything on your shoulders solely, when the weight could be shared, along with the joys of success. Yes, there are those rare few REALTORS® that have earned $1 million in real estate themselves, but typically it was very short lived and/or was due to a lucky year. This individual format generally cannot sustain high performance, leads to major swings in production, burn out, and eventual loss of income and market share.

The reward of working together as a cohesive unit can be greater than any profit gained while striving to be a solitary real estate agent on your own island. Even doctors work with medical clerks, nurses and anesthesiologists, while lawyer's teams consist of paralegals, junior attorneys and senior attorneys in today's society. Why would a customer work with an individual, sole practitioner agent when, for the same price, he can benefit from the advantages of hiring the whole team?

That's why we want to tell you about our 100 Deals system. Discover the real estate secrets for an easier, more enjoyable and more productive business, with time left over to enjoy your private life.

You're probably wondering, *"Who the hell are these guys?"* As real estate veterans, let us introduce ourselves.

I'm Rick Bengson, CEO and Co-Founder of ShowingSuite Inc. and Co-Creator of HomeFeedback.com.

I graduated from Northern Illinois University, went on to law school, and started in real estate in 1985 fresh out of college, working for one of the ten largest home building companies in the country. I began as a construction manager, moved into customer service, then into new home sales — I've built homes, I've serviced homes and I've sold hundreds of homes.

I started my love of technology as a member of the computer club in high school and began my major in 1981 in computer science. Back then Pong was big and we programmed on teletype machines without monitors. Although they were the only classes in which I received a rare "A," in my infinite wisdom I decided being a programmer was the only job in computers and that wasn't for me.

While working at my father's gas station, I read Tom Hopkins "How to Master the Art of Selling," and decided that selling was for me. I quit the family summer job and started on my sales path with Kirby vacuum cleaners. In my new summer job, I regularly was the top salesperson of the month at the age of 19 and 20. My boss said, *"Son, you have to be dumb enough to listen and smart enough to follow."* I did exactly what they said, where I saw the other sales people didn't.

After college, my first job was for a top 10 nationwide home builder in Phoenix. They hired educated people at a great pay with zero experience. I wanted to sell homes like Tom Hopkins, but their program was to teach you the entire home building business to run your own tract. My first position was as a construction manager building tract homes in Phoenix.

My first day on the job, I showed up in my required khaki pants, white shirt with company patch sewn on, and green hard hat. That morning, I arrived at the construction office, a converted office in the 30 plan model. I found my new boss Richard and asked him what I should do. He said, *"Go down to the cul-de-sac and find the other guys that look like you and they will get you started."* I answered, *"Ok thanks, I guess I will see you later."* I got back into my car and, being from a rural Illinois town, thought to myself, *"What's a cul-de-sac?"* I drove around the subdivision and eventually found the guys. I learned my first real estate term! One of the guys I found is now a bank president, whom I recently helped get on the board to open the bank. That first day they gave me ten homes under construction to build. Having never even built a tree house, this was quite an overwhelming task for this 21 year old. I persevered and figured it out. I remember finishing my first house and when the family moved in, I told my co-construction managers that I wanted to ring the doorbell and ask them, *"How do you like the house? It's my first one."* I never did and kept my job.

Needless to say you learn a lot when you are thrown into the fire feet first. I subsequently opened my own custom home building company a few years later. I sold my own spec homes and used technology to do so. I bought the first cell phone that wasn't installed in a car or in a bag to carry. It was a "brick" and I paid $1175 for it, but justified that if I could sell my houses faster, it more than paid for itself. I then moved from Scottsdale, Arizona to San Diego to live the California dream in real estate, where I now reside.

Since my beginning in real estate, I've been through three bad markets – the RTC crisis in Arizona, the military closures in San Diego in 1989 and the recent market. I still believe the San Diego market headed south the day I moved here that December day in 1989. I have experienced one good market starting in the late 1990's to 2007. I built dozens of custom homes in Scottsdale, completed numerous real estate projects in San Diego, and I have owned my current real estate brokerage for over the past ten years; therefore, I know how hard it can be. I've seen bust and boom, and right now the market is flat and expected to remain so for quite a while. Which is why we are sharing the system that works for closing 100 deals annually, no matter what. Bust, boom, or flat market conditions.

Of course, as a REALTOR®, a general rule is that you're getting paid a percentage of a sale, so when the prices are halved, you're making less money. But whatever the market, you should be able to live comfortably on 100 deals and that's why we've chosen this number as an achievable goal. Many teams achieve this goal — some even double it, triple it or more.

The reality is, when the market is better, you will do better. It's never going to stay the same condition forever. Regardless, 97%+ of all agents are never going to do 100 deals or $1 million a year in commissions. Some won't do 100 deals in their entire career, let alone every year. In fact, many REALTORS® will be asking, *"How the heck can an agent do 100 deals a year? I'm doing five a year."* That's what Alan brings to the table — he will explain the "real estate team concept" — how to build and maintain a team, and use technology to automate the processes of buying and selling homes.

Together, Alan and I developed Showing Suite, a real estate productivity software — it saves you time, helps you win listings over your competitors, and enables you to sell houses faster if you use the software. Originally entitled HomeFeedback. com Inc., we invented the concept of gathering feedback for real estate over the internet in 2000!

Previously, there was nothing available to provide the much-needed showing feedback from potential buyers to the REALTOR® and seller. So, Alan and I launched our first software product and sold the software now used by tens of thousands of agents in virtually every market in North America.

The technology that we created was a perfect fit with the expectations and revolutions happening throughout the rest of society. Although social networking sites and wireless devices are now the norm, back in the day, the majority of agents didn't even have email — at that time, the biggest seminar at the National Association of REALTORS® in 2000 when we launched was "how to use email." We constantly build onto the Showing Suite software as the business changes, so it will remain a much needed tool that agents can use throughout their career. We needed to keep up with the changing face of business and Alan had an idea how we could do this...

Licensed and selling homes since 1988, I'm Alan Shafran and I grew up in the industry.

My company, The Alan Shafran Group, sells 120-175 homes per year — averaging a sale every three days... in a market where the average agent sells fewer than

5 homes per year. I moved to Carlsbad, CA in 1999 and was among the top REALTORS® in the North County San Diego within 2 years. My license has been hanging with Prudential CA Realty for the majority of my career here in San Diego. I have been fortunate enough to be ranked their #1 highest producing REALTOR® in San Diego & North San Diego County for over 10 years and within the top 10 in North America for all of Prudential among over 60,000 other agents.

I have been privileged to speak across the country for different companies about what it takes to be successful and reach new heights in our industry. I have been honored to be included in different advisory boards including meetings at MIT for Prudential Corporate regarding technology direction. I also attribute much of my success to the wonderful people in this industry that helped me find the solutions to different pieces of the puzzle. Please realize this is a tough industry to attack on your own and I chose not to reinvent the wheel in many areas. Instead, I simply chose to surround myself with as much greatness as I could find.

Last, but certainly not least, my team is to whom I owe the most gratitude and respect. From a few of my agents who have been with me from near the start, to my office VP, to my admin, I will always be thankful. We continue to sell like clockwork, even though we've just been through what I think is a very rare time in real estate, and in the world in general. This recent economic crisis has indelibly impacted our future.

Over the past 22 years, I've been involved in three different geographical areas: Ventura County of Southern California (outside of L.A.); Denver, Colorado; and finally Carlsbad in San Diego County – very competitive markets, where I've had and maintained a very high level of success in a short period of time.

Certainly, this success is related to my team, but also to my economic background of managing money for PaineWebber, and my awareness of technological advances that can be used to automate and streamline our business today; they are leaps and bounds from what I started with.

For instance, in my first year in the business, nobody even had personal computers yet. We walked around with printed MLS books the size of The Yellow Pages Books – that's how much of a revolution I've been fortunate to be part of. I worked in an office with a hundred other agents and one modem-type terminal with a built-in dot matrix printer. When we needed to make a change to a home listing, we needed to fill out a printed sheet of paper and drive it over to the Multiple Listings Service; a week later, they would print the book with the changes in it.

Nowadays, of course, we have the internet, email, tablets like Apple's iPad and Motorola's Xoom, mobile devices and cell phones... Back then however, a REALTOR® was considered very forward thinking if they had an assistant and a pager.

Showing Suite was born out of my infatuation with technology. In the late '80s, early '90s, I would stay up until 2am, customizing databases for real estate. I was keen to use these early computer applications in the context of my business, so I was one of the first adopters of Windows – we went from DOS to Windows Networking, which was quite the challenge, but quite exciting to the geeky side of me.

I loved the latest gadgets and one day, I felt like I really understood this new world called the internet. So I wanted to build something to make my business better – as a result, we created what would become ShowingSuite.com which streamlined the whole process by saving us time and making everyone's lives better. Again, I chose to surround myself with great people and was fortunate enough run into Rick Bengson.

We are proud of ShowingSuite.com and the hundreds of thousands of agents that it has serviced over the years. Of course, we will always be gracious and thankful to our supporters and our clients within the industry. You will see us reference ShowingSuite.com and HomeFeedback.com throughout this book as an example of how technology can aid your mission in achieving your goals, both financially and personally for the quality of your life.

For over a decade, we have seen technology companies come and go, so we urge you to be careful when subscribing and putting your business into a company's hands. Do your research and make sure the company is the best option you have for now and the future. By understanding how ShowingSuite.com operates, we feel that you will be better educated in interviewing and identifying other fantastic technologies to help you with other areas of your business.

Nevertheless, I remember what it was like to do business with a customer 'pre-technology.' Sometimes we get lost in the fact that technology does everything for us and we forget about the customer. Truthfully, technology is helpful if it can solidify and make more efficient the relationship between the customer and us, their agents. It can also be helpful if it saves time automating tasks that would otherwise need to be done manually or could not be provided as a service without technology.

Through a team-based system, you can embrace the latest technology in order to facilitate communication in these important relationships – and not eliminate the relationships, which seems to be an unwelcome, yet typical side effect of impersonal emails and time-saving gadgets. We even built a specific team version in Showing Suite based on the needs of my business.

That's why this technology needs to be part of a broader system – one that supports the tech and is in turn, supported by it. Personally, I've been selling over 100 homes a year now for several years, through the different technologies and different markets. This amounts to roughly $17 million in income in the last 5-10 years.

I attribute this long-term success to insights – the tried and tested little secrets that can save you hundreds and thousands of dollars of expense and frustration – and my knowledge of the intricacies of team building and team relationships.

If you choose to listen to our advice, it is possible for you to rise up to the next level faster. But it's imperative that you keep your ego in check. I offer my time as a coach to fellow REALTORS® and you would be shocked by the things that I hear. For example, my coaching fees run between $2,000 and $3,000 per month for 30 minutes per week. One would think that for that price, a few things should naturally take place. The first few would be that the client should be asking questions, listening intently, and then implementing what they've learned. What actually happens would shock you. Most clients just want to talk and when they do ask a question and receive the answer, they would prefer to tell me why it can't be done. The egos are tremendous. For instance, a team leader who behaves like he's the big boss of GM, when he's actually running a small business or a family business; or a team member who sells a couple of houses and thinks he is God's gift to real estate.

Now, I love the concept of "thinking big," but one might steer themselves right out of business, making decisions like the CEO of GM when they are working out of their home office. Thinking big and dreaming big are fantastic and encouraged… let's combine it with a plan of action that includes solid decisions at correct growth intervals. I have found a tremendous inversive relationship between the team leader's ego and annual production. The production will not go up unless the ego gets out of the way.

Instead, always, always, and again, always put the customer first, and think about how you're being perceived. Not just public perception, but the perception of each other, is integral to building a team that works together dynamically and cooperatively.

🔑 You can think you are Superman when you do 20 deals a year, but ego could be your Kryptonite to reaching 100 deals if it is not kept in check.

By following a Blueprint for 100 Deals, my real estate firm has had very little staff turnover in several years. Some of you will already know that it's not uncommon to hire and fire employees every six months because of market volatility. You may sell three homes and hire a new team member, then it goes quiet for a while and you need to fire a person. However, I've learned how to develop a team, despite the troughs and peaks of this marketplace. By following and adhering to a system, you can effectively eliminate the volatility and benefit from the advantages of having a strong team on your side.

Just like I was an early trailblazer, you can adopt this Blueprint that Rick and I have created to blaze a trail of your own and grow your real estate business. My achievements speak for themselves and serve as perfect reasons for adopting a team philosophy in your real estate business, too.

Whether you're reading our book from the perspective of starting a team or becoming part of a team, it's imperative that you act now, because everything in the middle is going to get squeezed. Of course, not everyone wants to be a team leader (there are many hardships with the role, as well as benefits), and that's why we want to help you find the right direction and the best role for you on a team.

It's vital that the team fits together, works together, so they will inevitably succeed together!

There's more longevity to a team than the individual. So consider this: how do you want to grow your career? Do you want to be by yourself – where the tough days are tougher and the good days are solitary? Or do you want to be part of a team, working in unison to make a system work? There's support on the tough days, and celebrations on the good days with a team. Which situation do you think will have you suffering from burn-out more?

Throughout the book you will see certain paragraphs or sentences designated with a key icon 🔑 ; these are the "KEY 100." Think of them as the KEYS to your 100 deals – categories you will need to focus on to reach your goal. At the back of the book, these KEYS are copied or paraphrased for you to bookmark and refer to daily in order to stay on target towards your 100 deal goal.

We've done 100+ deals. Now you can, too. Grow as an individual, grow as a team, and grow as a business – it doesn't need to be lonely at the top, or a lonely ride to the top either!

Discover the Blueprint for 100 Deals...

Chapter 1
The Cardinal Rules of Real Estate

Real Estate Cheat Sheet

We're starting with the basics to give you a lay of the land – whether you're an experienced REALTOR® or relatively new to the real estate business. Either way, the priority for any agent or broker will be getting to know the critical marketing, communications and technology insights that enable you to sell houses faster and at the highest prices.

Markets go up and markets go down. That's why it's important to have a system that you can build for a long career in the business, providing you an abundance of business no matter the market. We rode an extremely hot market in most areas of the country from 2000-2007 and now we have new economic challenges, as we have faced an economic downturn that is the worse we have seen in 80 years.

It has widely been referred to as this generation's Great Depression. Economic fears were embedded in all buyers and sellers, which equates to a particularly difficult time for real estate agents. ⌐══ Hence, the great need for a system that works, whatever the condition of the economy; it's imperative to your long term success.

Knowing the Market

We, as agents, don't work on a nation-wide, state or regional basis. We work in our local markets where we service our clients. Although it's useful to know the real estate economic news on a more global basis, it is most important that you are well versed in your own market. Many markets, even through the recent crisis, did not experience a downturn, while others were devastated with as much as 60% depreciation.

Knowing your market may mean knowing that advertising in the local paper is a great bang for your buck, but in another market you could be burning hundred-dollar bills and need a different marketing avenue. Focus your business to meet the needs of your specific market. That may mean switching from representing a majority of buyers to representing 'short sale' sellers; it's always pretty obvious where the business is, and you need to adapt accordingly.

In down markets, the number of sales per agent quickly drops, until sales increase and/or agents drop out of the market. And, of course, as the number of sales drop so do housing prices due to the additional inventory this creates. Since we are mainly paid upon a percentage of the sales price of the homes that we sell; lower home prices mean lower commissions for agents like us. However, this also necessitates selling more homes in order to maintain our total compensation.

You may decide 50 is your magic comfort number or some may even build a team doing over 200 deals a year. Though, if you set a goal like 100 deals per year in your mindset, this could be the answer to your quest for a steady revenue stream, where your company can truly flourish into a year-after-year business that you can count on.

More Houses, Less REALTORS®?

As stated previously, the number of real estate agents declines as they are forced out of the business due to a housing slump. Naturally, every market cycle provides a cleansing of weaker real estate agents, making those who remain in the business poised to obtain more sales when the market recovers.

Other agents have had to change their focus, leaving the residential sales business and getting into property management, loan modifications or helping people find rentals. Yet, nothing can squelch the American dream of home ownership. And this growing inventory of homes won't sell themselves. Is this a time to panic? Or could it be a time for growth?

No matter the economy, some people buy. Of course, many consumers pull in their belts during uncertain economic times, although there are those who aren't impacted negatively by these downturns. While some people cut coupons, others buy mansions. **Are they buying from you?** That's the real question you need to be asking yourself.

Disaster or Opportunity?

For those who see the opportunities in life's twists and turns, a bad economy can lead to creating wealth – if you know what to do. Back during the Great Depression, there were savvy entrepreneurs and business people who made fortunes, simply by investing in real estate and waiting for boom times.

Those buyers are still out there, as well as those who will always want a home in which to raise their families. That's just the nature of life. And this is why now is a golden time of opportunity.

Still, in slow markets buyers are scarce and you must act with precision. Therefore, as your competition runs scattered and confused in the face of a changing landscape; you have the chance to make the right moves that will enable you to own your market for years to come – literally investing in your future.

Define Yourself by Success

In the words of Winston Churchill, *"Attitude is a little thing that makes a big difference."*

🔑 This is an ongoing tide of change, as we can never be 100% certain of market conditions, which is precisely why we need a system that isn't reliant on any particular economic landscape. Thus, throughout the economic highs and lows of tomorrow, there are ultimately only two options: **Stagnate** or **Grow.**

It's a no-brainer that if you are stagnating, you are no longer developing or progressing in your field; whereas, by growing, you are increasing in size and productivity. What makes better sense to you? Brokers can throw up their hands when faced with challenging external forces, or they can take action to maximize results – and profits.

Maximizing Your Business

🔑 For your practice to work, you must attract clients and provide value. Once again, this is true in any economy, up or down, you need to consistently grow your business and make it as successful as possible, in order to survive – and thrive!

You must:
• *Acquire more clients*

- *Keep in touch with existing clients so they call you when they need real estate services again*
- *When selling to new clients, you must let them know who you are and what value and benefits you can provide to them*
- *To be sure old clients return, you must make them both remember you and associate you with positive feelings through marketing and branding*

The secret to achieving these goals and growing your real estate business, no matter the economy, is **adjusting your mindset and setting up efficient sustainable systems, which can be executed quickly and conveniently.**

If you can focus your mindset on Forward-Thinking then you can move with the changes that are necessary, and which need to be applied to every area of your business – Client Growth, Customer Service, Marketing, etc.

Naturally, this is a challenge. Yet, by using the technological advances that are specifically developed for the real estate vertical market, it's possible to put in place, gain support from, and maintain a competitive edge, via the systems and processes that will put you far ahead of your competition.

Technology
We have seen that real estate agents spend an inordinate amount of time in administrative tasks that have little to do with selling. However, by putting efficient technology into place, you can drastically increase your productivity and achieve 100 Deals each and every year.

National Association of REALTORS® past President, Thomas M. Stevens says, *"The real estate industry today bears little resemblance to the way we did business 10 years ago. It is hard to find another industry that has adopted technology so readily to its customers."*

⌕ You don't need to be a "Techie" to use technology. If you are not comfortable using technology and are more of a face time person than a Facebook person, this does not have to be a barrier for you to provide tech for your clients that require it. Know this is a blind spot of yours and seek help. Align yourself with a brokerage that is tech savvy, has automated systems in place and does this for you, or perhaps your first hire is a tech savvy team administrator or intern to help you. Others can do all of this for you and you can list and sell homes.

☞ **Here are the top 5 benefits of technology under our Blueprint for 100 Deals system:**

1. Streamlining

Today, online technology can streamline and in many cases completely perform real estate agents' necessary but repetitive and thankless tasks, enabling agents to focus on what they do best – dealing with the actual customers and selling homes!

It's not about working harder to increase your profits – it's about working smarter. And this is where **automation** can take you one step ahead (or at least level the playing field and bring you up to speed with your competitors).

For example, emails seeking feedback that are sent automatically to showing agents raise response rates from 20% to at least 70%. When showing agents don't respond, follow-up emails can be sent automatically.

Moreover, it is critical to capture leads and nurture them. All this can be done automatically while the contact appears personalized.

Other Automation Tips:

A calendaring system that is easy to use and automatically informs sellers of showings via email saves on time and mistakes. Integrate your software whenever possible to avoid re-keying data and to expedite automating tasks. Companies report that providing the integrated software to their workers boosts productivity by 20%.

Look for what we call "one touch" systems and tools. Essentially, it is exactly what it sounds like. You take all the tasks that your job is composed of, and systemize them with both technology and staff into a system that only requires you to touch it one time. Obviously, it's not possible with every aspect of our industry… but it certainly is our goal!

Many technology tips will follow in the Chapters ahead…

2. Real Time

Thanks to technology, it's possible for you and sellers to have 24/7 access to critical information. An agent who has their operation set up so that a seller can go to a website at any time and review the latest showings and feedback has a huge edge over their competition – not to mention, they will have access to a wealth of real-time data to help them react quickly and do their jobs better, and sell more homes!

For instance, if you've ever had to ask a seller to lower the price of an overpriced home, you know how difficult it can be. It's hard to get sellers to be realistic, or even get them to repaint that fuchsia living room.

Usually, when you tell them to lower the price or repaint to a neutral color, they look at you skeptically and wonder if they should have hired another agent. That is until you can show them actual quantitative, current, and objective feedback from the prospective buyers who are turned off by the price, smell or color. This allows for real time reactions/solutions to real time issues.

You can also use real time systems for prospects to search listings, obtain home valuations, receive neighborhood data, etc.

3. Flexibility
Being nimble is critical in this environment, and technology is the key to keeping your finger on the pulse of your customers. Not to mention that a business should be able to change directions as fast as a speedboat; this flexibility is crucial as a slow-turning cruise ship will be left behind.

Whether you're dealing with short sales and foreclosures, or trying to win-out on multiple offers, in every market speed matters. You need to constantly update along with the technology to stay quick, nimble and flexible, to get as many sellers as you can in a fast market, and as many buyers as you can in a slow market.

4. High Profile
Technology can help you to maintain a profile. Through your website, social media websites and applications that presently exist, from blogs to Facebook, to Twitter and mobile solutions you can keep clients in the loop on your achievements, raise your public image on the 'web', and remain in their mind's eye as a leader in your market.

This constantly updating 'image' of you and your business leads into the next point, which is...

5. Transparency
Part of moving forward is transparency – Technology that is easy to use and makes the real estate process more transparent impresses buyers, sellers and asset managers.

In a business where previously the norm was zero transparency when we actually held printed MLS listing books that were specifically kept from the public, we're now expected to be 100% transparent and provide access to all information, from listings to feedback, to escrow fees.

In the present and future, transparency encourages REALTORS® to be completely forthcoming about what showings have happened on a house, not to mention disclosing every marketing aspect that you've attempted to help sell the property.

Ultimately, agents have lost a lot of control and privacy, and they're under more scrutiny than before. But, this aspect is also good for consumer trust, as they know that we're accountable and they appreciate this open business approach.

Another offshoot of this transparency is websites like Yelp, where customers can review your business and post their comments. It's a trend of the times that everyone will know, and want to know, how many deals you've done, what size, etc. Prospective buyers and sellers will be able to see every transaction you've ever completed, and even rate your performance online. You should be ready for that and even start conducting your business with a forward-thinking, transparent style.

Keeping Up

Naturally, many REALTORS® today are fatigued by some of these social sites and have asked us, how much time do you have to spend blogging, or Facebooking or Tweeting? Keeping pace with the technology can be very challenging and it's okay to wonder how can someone keep up with all this change and still do our actual job of selling homes. It can be a daunting task, juggling showings and keeping up with the social media side of things. (We will cover social media more in Chapter 5).

Ultimately, the bottom line is that all these developments are going to get you business, but the trick is leveraging it, while automating where possible to keep it manageable in the long-run. Regardless, it's clear that you can't just sit back on your heels and do what you used to do even 2-3 years ago, because change is happening so fast. You can't rest on our laurels, or your business won't grow; it's going to be stagnant.

The days of simply sending out mailers, running classified ads, newspaper display ads and home magazine ads are over. Dependent upon your market, it's possible to continue these timeless tactics, but that's not enough. Unless your intent is to use this media as a method to direct prospects to your website or landing page for lead capture, then it probably does not make sense to invest your first advertising $ in that direction.

Of course, if you have the funds, then mailers, billboards and newspapers are for those who have already invested in those arenas and continue to get the returns to outpace those costs. Yet, those returns are diminishing quarter after quarter. ⌐━➤ Do not invest in these media unless you are already receiving positive cash flow from them. You should be shifting your model towards doing all of your business online. Moving with this trend is proactive and wise.

⌐━➤ We must align ourselves with good brokerage and technology companies that are similarly forward-thinking and let them do the work for us. We must apply an open-minded direction to ensure that we're current and ever-changing with the conditions and temperament of the marketplace. As a result, we can remain even keeled in any economy.

Without a forward-thinking mindset, it would be impossible to stay atop and keep riding this wave of change in the industry.

So, you've made it this far: you're on your board, and aware of some of the waves and wipeouts inherent in opening and running a real estate business – and the technology and mindset that will keep you afloat for years to come.

Now it's time to delve deeper into the 100 Deals system…

__Read on… Chapter 2: Why Stop at 100?__

Chapter 2
Why Stop at 100?

One hundred might seem like an arbitrary number, and it is. Yet, from our experience, it's also an ideal milestone for real estate professionals looking for a more stable and productive business environment.

Still you may wonder, why not 50? Why not 200? Certainly, 100 is not the pinnacle and you shouldn't feel bound to stick rigidly to this number by any means. However, 100 is our recommendation as a working blueprint for success; let us explain why that is...

First, what is your ultimate goal for your real estate career?
We assume that you want to make significant money to improve your standard of living and create a successful business, with as minimal headaches and disruptions as possible. That's where 100 becomes a magic number in this equation – we have found that a minimum of 100 deals a year generates significant income, without stressing and worrying about the highs and lows of market conditions.

A typical REALTOR® hits the 4 to 6 mark, in an average year, and less than this in a major downturn. Depending on the geographic and economic market conditions, the average sale price sits around $300,000 per home. Therefore an agent may survive on 4 to 6 deals but when conditions worsen and that turns into 2 to 4 deals, bills cannot be met and another steadier source of income is immediately looked for and henceforth, the dream of selling real estate is over.

Meanwhile, some REALTORS® will manage approximately 20 deals in the same amount of time, and be considered a 'big producer.' Nevertheless, what we've discovered is the REALTOR® who is selling in the region of 40 to 50 homes is actually working twice as hard as someone closing 100 deals. Instead of working double-time as logic dictates, 100 deals is the answer to an easier and more profitable working life for you.

How is this possible?

Well, basically, at any number lower than 100, you're simply not creating enough leads or revenue to support a larger team in your office and – in a vicious cycle – because you have less staff, you are limited in the opportunities available to you. Thus, you are hitting an invisible wall in the real estate biz – you can't reach the 100 milestone as you don't currently earn enough money to execute consistent, effective marketing, and, at the same time, hire the right administrative staff. Because you don't have the personnel to handle and coordinate 100 deals, you can't earn enough money to sustain the staff that you need on your team... And round and round we go!

Essentially, you're holding yourself back – and that means you're stuck in a rut where you're doing most of the work.

How do you break through this wall?

It seems unsurpassable. An impasse to your future success as a REALTOR®. That wall of 10 deals needs to be broken through, then the 25 deals' wall milestone, then the 50 deals wall milestone, and then onwards if you're to reach your optimal performance level of 100 deals.

Like a long distance runner, sometimes you hit a 'wall' and need to run until you smash down this virtual barrier, and then the endorphins kick in and you reach that next level of energy – to keep going, and win the race. After you start to hit these deal milestones and look back you will surprise yourself that you ever did that few deals a year in the subsequent years to come.

Truly, once you reach 40 to 50 deals a year, it is one of the toughest places to be. Usually you're putting in 12-14 hours a day – it requires all those extra hours from the leader; this is time spent away from making those deals! And there's extra spending all round, yet you don't see the big profit.

The low cycles are tougher, because it means cutting the spending and saying goodbye to some of your staff. And then things ramp up again, so you kick it into gear, and you hire the admin and marketing all over again. But, when that low cycle inevitably returns, team members are fired, spending is cut, and you're constantly resetting to where you originally started.

This cycle exists whether it's a new agent, with zero deals to their name, all the way up to those agents in the 40 to 50 range. You're starting and stalling in this awful cyclical pattern, but it needn't be this way.

Although, unfortunately, the ground isn't much more stable in between 50 and 100 either – in fact, we rarely see any agents in this shaky 'dead-zone' between the 50s and the next league of REALTORS® in the 100 zone.

After you reach 50 deals in your past 12 months, set yourself a salary that you can pay your current staff, office, marketing, and living expenses and not a dollar more. For the following 12 months reinvest all of your profits back into your business. What to spend those monies on will be addressed later, but here is a quick breakdown of what you need to spend your excess NOI (Net Operating Income) on:

- *Fill your staff with the quality personnel you need*
- *Marketing – websites, SEO, mobile exposure, PPC, social, print*
- *Smart technology – web based "cloud" software to build and manage your business*
- *Enhance client services – unique services you offer, transparency solutions to build trust*
- *Image improvement – office location, office furniture and signage, presentation room, logo upgrade*

Why make this sacrifice? Because at 100 deals, it's a sweet spot where the low cycles are less and high cycles are more. Once you manage to break through this wall, you 'glide' to 100. Your costs will remain more fixed and the staff you can make a significant profit with at 100 deals can nearly be the same size to do 150 – 175 deals.

Of course, breaking through the glass ceiling to reach the top isn't something you can do without changing your game. You can't do this on your own; you need the support of a team.

Do's and Don'ts of Getting to 100

Do Go for 100; Don't Stretch Your Limits...
While we believe that one can accomplish anything, and to go for your dreams, we also believe that life can pass by quickly and quality is as important as quantity. We believe in reaching our goals and maintaining an incredible lifestyle that encourages family time, personal time, hobbies, vacations, etc. With that said, we advise to be aware of the limits of yourself and your team. 100 deals aren't born overnight. It requires a mindset and a method, which is implemented each and every day.

Put a cap on it. Don't reach for 200 deals; make 100 your lucky number, because this is also about not stretching yourself too thin. Otherwise you're back to where you started. For instance, if you have a team of four reaching for 200, you will be compromising customer service and failing miserably.

Don't try to build a team, or go for 100, without a clear cut plan...
Without a solid blueprint, without proper budget levels built-in, without an idea of who you need on your team, you're literally flying blind and the results will be equally hit or miss.

It's possible to get there, without giving up the world, but it has to be well executed.

Don't 'buy' a team...
This isn't worthwhile or rewarding in the long run. In case you're unsure of the concept of buying agents, take this hypothetical example: a real estate office offers to pay a new agent 50% of a commission, and an experienced agent might get 90%. Because of that mentality, many team leaders have bought agents, saying: 'Okay, I'll give you 75-80% for every deal you bring in.'

Yet, at 20-25% coming to you, what happens is you don't actually make enough money from the transaction to invest it back into the business. Therefore everyone loses in the long run, as the team leader no longer has the funds to withstand the cycles that we've discussed earlier while maintaining the marketing and staff necessary to keep the 100 deal minimum. As a result, this process becomes more about ego than running a decent business.

Do have the right attitude...
Roll with the times or be left behind — look to the future by upgrading to the latest revolutions in IT, keeping that all important mindset devoted to moving forward.

The right attitude also means setting aside the ego — don't let it rule you or your business, then you'll be focused on what really matters: building and keeping a team that allows you to reach your goals.

100 Deals = How Many on Your Team?

So, now we're aiming for 100; how many team members do you need to effectively and efficiently reach this new deal level? How many team members will make this an achievable goal, and help you to develop and maintain the well-oiled machinery that will keep your business running smoothly?

It's a balancing act, no question about it. Too many team members are unnecessary; too few and you will be hindered in performance.

It may take some time to figure out the perfect number for your team, as every real estate business is different. Though, as a rough guideline, the size of a team for 100 deals is a minimum of 6 to 7 key players — this would probably be 4 sales people (including the leader) and 3 administrative personnel.

But don't be fooled into thinking that a team of 100 means you'll do a THOUSAND deals — it's more about striking that fine balance where your team is functioning at its optimum level.

The fact of the matter is, there are a lot of teams that fail… if not most of them. It's not uncommon to see a team of 8 to 9 people, and they're only doing 10 or 20 transactions a year. Size doesn't guarantee success. There are many people who think they just need to fill their office with bodies and it will automatically increase business. But, in real estate, that's just not the case.

Therefore, what is just as critical as building a team that is the right size (and with the right people on board) is building a team that is efficient. You need to have tabs on these people and transparency within your business to know what's going on, in order to ensure it's effective and well-organized.

Furthermore, just like any business, your team needs to be built on the right columns — or else, what happens is you've built this team that's extracting so much energy in the wrong directions, they can't possibly move forward.

Of course, it's easy to talk about the importance of putting together your team and creating these strong foundations. In actuality, it won't be as easy as ABC, but we will walk you through the next steps to implement a blueprint for making this happen. But, right now, the first step is realizing that having a good team will be critical to your long-term success.

At this volume of turning around 100 homes, you can keep your business and systems running to the point where you have rainmaker systems that don't depend on any one individual.

Your Team & Technology – The Secret to Reaching 100 Deals (Year After Year)

> *"The number one benefit of information technology is that it empowers people to do what they want to do. It lets people be creative. It lets people be productive... It is all about potential."*
>   - Steve Ballmer, CEO, Microsoft

Ultimately, getting to 100 requires team work <u>and</u> technology. Without these key components, your recipe for success is lacking one or all of the most important ingredients.

As we've addressed, 100 deals is inextricably connected to having a team, and vice versa. You can't do one without the other.

This is the core concept at the heart of our book – by having a team or being part of a great team, you and your business will benefit overall.

You may already be aware that, as REALTORS®, our roles and responsibilities are becoming increasingly transparent; liabilities continue to rise; accountability continues to rise; consumer's knowledge and demand for service, and our availability, also continues to rise. As a result, it's less and less realistic that a consumer would hire a single agent to do the whole job, as opposed to hiring a team of agents. Bottom line, they just wouldn't be getting as much bang for their buck. And you can bet that continued transparency will educate consumers accordingly.

Thus, one of the secrets to utilizing technology and your team, to their maximum levels of efficiency and effectiveness, is **Administration**. Through the automation side of technology and the basics of having admin staff that can pick up the phone for you, you can save valuable time, energy and money.

By combining the powers of technology with the proper amount of hands-on administration, you will be taking the right track to reaching your new target of 100 deals.

Consider the cost benefits, for instance. Did you know that, when using automated technology properly, you can save the full annual salary of a staff member!

For instance, Showing Suite's system will cost you as little as a few hundred dollars a year, versus the salary of an extra admin assistant in the ballpark of $20,000-$35,000 a year.

Naturally, you need to be forward-thinking to move with the times and embrace these technological upgrades. But, unfortunately, many brokers across the country just don't earn enough off their sales people to help them re-invest. If agents are depending on this broker to provide them with the best tools and technologies, they can expect to be disappointed. Fact is, brokers don't make a lot of money after paying their rent and overheads. Truly, they would need to bring in millions to generate any kind of real significant profit.

It's a shame because, with these automation savings, you could spend the extra cash on your business instead – investing in the company's team and technology. But, that doesn't mean you can operate with zero staff in your office. That's not the point of automation. Instead, a modest reduction from 5 to, say, 4 admin staff is generally what we would expect. This can result in your saving an annual salary, due to the technology, without sacrificing the human touch of these team members who will be invaluable along the road to 100 deals. Imagine what you could spend an extra $3,000 – $4,000 a month on your business with the monies saved via technology.

Yet, who should be on your admin team? What role will they play? And who are the essential team members for your team?

Alternatively, if you're interested in enhancing your value as a team member, or joining a team that would benefit you, what qualities should you be looking for in yourself and your team mates?

Read on... Chapter 3: Dream Team 100

Chapter 3
Dream Team 100

"Individual commitment to a group effort – that is what makes a team work, a company work, a society work, a civilization work."
— Vince Lombardi

In building our Blueprint for 100 Deals, the Team is undoubtedly the most critical architecture to put into place. Each team member will play their role as a vital cog in the machinery of your real estate business. The administrational members of your team will act as the backbone, and the sales agents will be the life blood, which – when working together as a strong cohesive unit – will take you and your 'Dream Team' to the top.

Advantages of Being on a Team

For the lone wolves who once prowled the industry alone, the benefits of joining a team will be already apparent, or the differences will become clear quickly. Yet, for those who are new to real estate, the team advantage might not be so obvious.

In the beginning, you may have entered into real estate because you wanted independence and may prefer not to work with others. In fact, in some ways, a team may seem a cumbersome approach, with accountability and many people to coordinate with, and a drain on your earnings. This is, of course, short-sighted and the following benefits are actually part and parcel of being on a (good) team:

- *Play to your strengths* – *You can focus on what you're good at, or you enjoy doing, while delegating admin tasks, enabling you to close more deals.*
- *Share the burdens/successes* – *Celebrating as part of a team is better than celebrating on your own; the same can be said of failures which can also be commiserated together. Thus, a team environment makes these highs and lows seem smoother and less impactful on the overall big picture of your business.*
- *Share the costs/overheads* – *Rather than shelling out money to start up or maintain your real estate business, there may be a team in your area which would benefit from your abilities and value the skills you bring to the table.*
- *Balanced life* – *By adding more staff members to the equation, the result should also be a healthier, more balanced life, with extra time for your family and yourself, instead of burning out trying to accomplish enough deals as a solo agent practitioner.*
- *You can actually achieve* 100 *deals* – *Without the team backing you up, quite frankly it's near impossible to make it to our goal of 100 deals, and certainly impossible to sustain it (without jeopardizing your own health and that delicate work-life balance).*
- *Marketing and staff benefits* – *You get the benefits of marketing and staff without the upfront cash out of your pocket. When the team has a bad month and low income, typically the team leader is the one who has to pull cash out of pocket to pay for the overhead. While the team member gets to keep the profit from all of their personal transactions contributed to the team.*

Whatever level of the business interests you, because the industry has changed, it's a perfect time for a brand new person to now get involved in real estate. But, you need to think about the role that you will play on a team.

In the words of Tom Ferry, renowned real estate coach and speaker: *"Either be the team leader... or join a team... it's the future of our industry."*

What Team Member Are You?

There are numerous players on a team. Whether you are planning who you might need onboard, or you're assessing what part you will play on an existing team, here are descriptions of the key personnel that are essential for a successful real estate business.

President/CEO

This person is the head of the group. He/she needs to be passionate about building the business and the team. A good President and CEO is somebody who is 100% committed to the cause. They're willing to take on the liability and hopefully receive the reward of the risk-taking as well.

This player is also usually the best sales person on the team. That's where a big chunk of teams fail today; the CEO needs to have been, at one point or time, an excellent REALTOR®. The CEO needs to understand and be excellent at almost every facet of the business, every negotiation aspect of the business, and be willing to train the team in the appropriate skill sets necessary for their position.

For the President, running a team can be like running a Doctor's office – you're the head person with several specialist partners and staff.

VP/Manager

The second in command, the VP or Team Manager needs to be fantastic at managing an administrative team. This requires them to be very diligent, very organized and very efficient. We find this position is probably the key element to continuity of the team, consistency of the sales agents, and staff efficiency. This person should be fantastic at what the CEO is not… which typically is staff and people management. Most team leaders don't have the tolerance and or patience for their team's dramatic periods. Yet dealing with those situations and team conflicts in a patient and respectful manner, is absolutely critical and necessary.

Moreover, a manager should be good at blending the sales and the administration sides of the business, and the people side of the business.

There is plenty of juggling involved; imagine you've got your admin staff (3 or 4 people) and each one has their own unique drama and problems. The Team Manager listens and calms them down, which is key to keeping long-term staff members who are happy, productive and valuable.

Essentially, a Team Manager understands how people work, and realizes that sales people are different animals – they need to be kept accountable to the business and yet still have a feeling of independence.

That's why running these teams isn't an easy line to walk, as you will be constantly challenged by both sides – the admin and the sales staff.

Of course, everyone sets out to have a successful team; whether there's 20 people on a team, or just 2 people, there will occasionally be someone upset or having issues. This needs to be managed and maintained to get the best out of the team as a whole. Hence the importance of these leaders at the top, and why we need to trust what they're doing.

Receptionist/Call Coordinator

This is the voice that most clients will hear first — the receptionist is one of the team players that is often underpaid and given less credit than they deserve. If anything, the receptionist should be overpaid! It's not an easy job, having to smile and be nice — no matter what. This person can also be the office cheerleader, lifting internal spirits on days the team needs the help.

Listing Assistants

These are the administration staff that help facilitate the listings process. They assist with the preparation of paperwork prior to a listing appointment, and help prepare contracts once a listing is taken. They may even help with comparables and everything in between — from photos of homes to flyers, to providing feedback, to gathering data and compiling info. Their duties might also include the process of making sure that listings are serviced properly until sale. The goal is always: *under promise, over service*. Being extra attentive will ensure happy customers.

In House Transaction Assistant or Escrow Manager

This assistant is also critical to reach 100 deals. The advantage to having an in house person vs. outsourcing is the hand held care the clients receive. This hand holding and personal care leads to better service, better experiences, and eventually more referrals and repeat customers. Also, and depending on the assistant's skill sets, they may also take a stronger role in negotiation of offers, physical inspections, appraisals, etc. Of course, we recommend that all assistants be licensed in the state in which your office resides.

Buyer Agents

The listing assistants take on some of the work that can typically distract Buyer Agents. These are your sales staff and many of them will still have that lone wolf mentality, and it's this independent spirit that makes them good at their jobs. But, the mindset should be moving towards a team focus, working together to reach the ultimate goal of 100 deals.

If you break it down, the main agent is the CEO/leader of the company, then one to three agents on staff, and a listing assistant who handles the admin details. Depending on the size of your business, and how many listings you are handling, this will ascertain how many agents and listing assistants you need on your team.

For instance, one assistant can handle 50 listings when each listing is worth approximately $50,000 a piece. Yet, if you look at a luxury market like La Jolla in San Diego, the average listing is $2.5 million; a listing assistant wouldn't want to take on much more than 20 listings in this scenario. This is due to the amount of hand-holding that is required in this type of market, where viewings are scheduled manually and the customers expect extra time and attention for their money.

Other Staff:
Transaction Coordinator or Assistant
Depending on the jurisdiction, either a "neutral" transaction coordinator or two attorneys (one for each side) will be dealing with escrow arrangements. They coordinate legal paperwork between parties involved, yet their role can be outsourced at the beginning of your business.

Marketing
This role may also be outsourced if yours is a small team, although as your real estate business grows, there might be a need for an in-house Marketer. They handle the cold-calling of past clients, expired listings and 'for sale by owners,' trying to drum up business. All people making sales calls and contacts should be licensed, before any REALTOR® activities.

Virtual Assistants
This is someone who can assist you from an off-site 'virtual' location, instead of having them in your office. For example, Showing Suite is a type of virtual assistant, which replaces some of the tasks required of your staff.

A Virtual Assistant is the first step to building a team if you are currently an agent looking to expand. First you would want a virtual staff member for 15 hours a week, to get the ball rolling, as it's a great way to expand while keeping low overheads. One can also hire full time virtual assistants out of other countries like the Philippines, using Skype and similar methods to communicate. There are challenges of course, but then again, a full time employee for a total cost of $1,300 per month is a bargain compared to most U.S. employment markets.

Runners, part-time people
Outside of the typical admin roles, there may also be part-time 'runners' for errands and delivering packages, as well as 'sign placers' (who place Open House signs).

These positions are market driven and depend on the size of your geographic scope.

Typically, most admin staff have dreams of being a REALTOR®, and they want to learn the ropes from the inside. The other type of admin staff member is usually a former REALTOR® who wants to keep a hand in the business in their twilight years or to have a more consistent contribution to their family.

 *Technology*

Think of technology as part of your team. Technology is cheap compared to personnel. You need to have systems that will replace mundane tasks and save time for team members. To learn more, we will look at the technical systems which can assist your team in Chapter 6.

Business Relationships

Some interactions and relationships are utilized on a 'per transaction' basis. It's important to develop these contacts, so your team can call upon these players, as required:

- *Inspections & repairs*
- *Appraisals*
- *Loan issues*
- *Contingencies*
- *Coop Agent*

Psychology of the Team

The psychology of working as a team, versus an individual, is much more complex, yet worth understanding – whichever role you are playing in the team; no matter if you're leading, buying/selling or administrating.

It's a distinct change in mentality, going from a tennis singles player's individual mindset of alone vs. their opponent, to that of a tennis double player's mindset of being on the same side of the court and playing as part of an integrated team. The mindset of a team is all about "the whole being worth more than just the sum of its parts."

When working alone you might reach 20 deals if you work really hard at it, but together your combined efforts can take you to 100 and you will net more dollars after costs per transaction. However, everyone needs to be onboard with this common goal, and be willing to put the 'work' into teamwork.

To function as a team, first they must think like a team. Like fingers on a hand, if one is not moving, the hand's actions are lessened and the results are more difficult to obtain.

Get Goosed!

Think of the goose – Geese work together to make them stronger, as you should to make your goals more achievable. Every flap of a goose's wing creates uplift for the bird following directly behind. This is why geese fly in a V-formation. It's teamwork and it works.

Other lessons from geese include their technique of taking turns being at the front of the V, to curb fatigue and keep the team strong and focused. Furthermore, the geese at the back of the V constantly 'honk' to encourage the other geese to keep up their speed. Remember these lessons when giving praise and words of encouragement to your team mates, and when sharing the hard work of your business to make your team stronger and more successful.

Building a Team

Although there isn't an exact science or mathematic formula for calculating the perfect team size that will guarantee making it to the milestone of 100 transactions per year, we can provide our own personal anecdotal experience for building that ideal team.

 Alan's Recipe for 100+ Deals Success:

Team Players:

> *1 Team Manager*
> *4 Buyers Agents (at a minimum)*
> *3 Admin Assistants*

Result: 100+ transactions a year

In the beginning, I was doing 50 deals, and my team consisted of two buyer agents, two admin staff, and myself. Then I grew the team accordingly, and I now reach a total of 120 or more deals a year. Nevertheless, with the advent of technology, it's possible to do 180 deals with four assistants and five buyer agents. This is exciting leverage to use for your advantage.

Defining the Team

The definition of a 'team' is a group of people linked in a common purpose; a team is organized to work together interdependently and cooperatively to meet the needs of their customers. But, the types of teams that exist under this umbrella term are varied.

Different Types of Teams

Big or small? What works for you? We can't answer that question, but you should know some of the potential issues with a partnership of just two agents (as opposed to a larger team with admin staff, too).

Of course, it might not seem like 2 people are a 'team', but any number of agents who share commissions and enter into a contract together are part of a team. Yet, invariably, when working in a duo, one agent is carrying more weight than the other. As a result, this agent becomes jaded and disappointed, and ultimately begins to search for a bigger team to share the weight, or cuts loose the 'dead weight' of the other agent.

While it's possible there are exceptions to this rule of working in a twosome, the focus needs to be reaching 100 to maximize your efforts, instead of burning out and languishing at 50 deals or less. This ultimately means seeking a team with a number greater than two.

Nevertheless, while two is naturally the minimum number for a team, there are some teams that are so large that they even diversify into spin-off services, such as mortgage brokering or loaning out moving vans to customers. Yet, once again, we recommend keeping your eye on the prize – the main focus has to be staying on target for those 100 deals.

Hiring and Budgeting for a Team

If you've decided that you would like to expand your business by building a new or larger team – as opposed to joining an existing team – then, as we've recommended, a Virtual Assistant is a low-cost way to start the process.

Yet, you will also be wondering about the budget as you add new staff members to your payroll. Essentially, it's a case of needing to spend money and invest in your team financially, in order to make money and reach the next plateau of 100 transactions.

This boost is about an extra push to the top, while many are stuck in a rut, because in order to go that extra mile, you need to enlarge your team.

Maintaining and Keeping a Team

🔑 *"Highly productive people are attracted to highly productive offices."*

- Carol Johnson,
President of The Recruiting Network Inc.

Just as important as building a team that can function in a well-oiled and professionally efficient manner, is maintaining these cogs to ensure you can continue on the right track. This means a happy team, which will function well in the long-run, not just in the short term – after all, we want to hit 100 transactions every year, year after year.

Naturally, there will be turnover. It's a fact of life. You're going to go through some people – not every first fit is the right fit. You can expect friction amongst certain team members, and you will need to constantly assess if this friction requires maintenance, or correction by removing the 'squeaky wheel' that requires too much grease in this analogy.

As we've mentioned before, if every team member (including yourself) can check their ego at the door, you will be on course for staying on track with the essence of the word 'Team', and not 'Monarchy.' Certainly, your role is critical, but so is theirs. Therefore, make sure everyone's ego is boosted properly and, vice versa, kept in check.

For example, encourage the concept of Partnership. We operate under the ideology: *"As Team Manager, I am a Senior Partner, and my fellow agents are Junior Partners."* They work with you, not work for you. When it's the latter, team members feel undervalued and they appear inexperienced in the eyes of the clients who view them as subordinates not equals.

Furthermore, this takes a huge load off your shoulders if the client wants to work with your team members and not just you personally. Otherwise, everything shuts down when you go on a vacation, for example...

🔑 Ultimately, this is all about building a team and a sustainable business. Investing in the players on your team is the secret to success.

Building the Team Culture

"Coaches who can outline plays on a blackboard are a dime a dozen. The ones who win get inside their players and motivate."
– Vince Lombardi

Team Communication

A large part of maintaining and keeping your team is communication. We recommend that you leave your door open figuratively and literally, and that you communicate regularly with staff members.

Just as we noted in the description of the Team Manager's role, he or she will be communicating with the CEO and the other team members on a daily basis. This is a vital chain of communication for sharing and solving problems before they erupt, addressing concerns before they become major issues, and listening to new ideas and improvements from each level of the real estate business.

Most importantly, this style of cohesive and collaborative communication will encourage an open and approachable relationship with clients, and equally with the team, who will be better connected to what customers want and need – thus improving the business and increasing the success rates.

__Read on... Chapter 4: Communication / Bandwidth__

Chapter 4
Communication / Bandwidth

"In business, communication is everything."
– Robert Kent, former Dean, Harvard Business School

Without good communication, you don't have a business. Whether you're staying in touch via telephone, face-to-face, IM, text or email; communication is the interpersonal 'glue' that holds everything together, cementing the foundations of your team, and sealing every crack to create a seamless and cohesive unit.

By paying close attention to what you say and how you say it, this communication aspect of being a REALTOR® is vital in perfecting your sales relationships with other agents and the clients who buy and sell homes.

There are many unique relationships involved in each of the 100 transactions of your growing business. These will require excellent communications between the Listing Agent and Showing Agents, the Agent and Seller, the Agent and Buyer, and the Agents on the team in your office.

Fundamentally, without taking the initiative to improve and maintain high standards of communication, any business will fall apart. Yet, communication is especially important in real estate. There needs to be ongoing team work and you need to keep customers in the loop, and happy, at all times.

Communication Tools

If you want to have any hope of creating a business that can successfully achieve 100 deals then, absolutely, communication is one of the most important building blocks.

Email, direct mail, word of mouth, and telemarketing – these are the tools in your arsenal. Like any well-equipped tool box, you should use all of these tools together to get the job done, but always consider where to put your emphasis.

When asked to rate the effectiveness of marketing tools, using a sliding scale, real estate agents concluded the following, with 1 = extremely ineffective and 5 = extremely effective:

- *Word of Mouth (referrals): 4.52*
- *Personal Sales: 4.05*
- *Email: 3.72*
- *Direct Mail: 2.89*
- *Signage: 2.33*
- *Telemarketing: 2.04*
  (Source: Investigating Media Effectiveness in Residential Real Estate Marketing: The Agent's Perspective.)

Utilized together, these comprehensive tools will help to market and drive your business through active communication.

Good Communication is Good Business?

- *Yes, good communication means drastically increased revenue.*
- *Effective communication is a leading indicator of financial performance.*
- *Companies that communicate effectively significantly outperform their peers.*
- *Companies with effective internal communications show 57 % higher shareholder return compared with organizations with less effective internal communications (stats from Watson Wyatt, Communication ROI Study, Communication World, May/June 2008).*
- *Agencies that communicate effectively are 4.5 times more likely to report high levels of worker engagement.*
- *According to Gallup polls, workers who have an above-average attitude toward their work generate 38% higher customer satisfaction scores, 22% higher productivity, and 27% higher profits for their companies (Source: Here Today, Here Tomorrow: Transforming Your Workforce from High-turn-over to High-Retention, Gregory Smith, 2005)*

What is Good Communication?

Communication in real estate needs to be often, it needs to be flexible to accommodate the client's lifestyle and characteristics, and it needs to be efficient.

Client Communication – Success Requires Transparency

Communication with clients today hinges largely on the **transparency that you provide them.** This transparency is basically giving clients the ability to see what's actually going on with the purchase or sale of their home.

In our marketplace, sellers are increasingly demanding a transparent relationship. They want to know what you are doing to sell their house. They want to be informed during every step of the process or they would like to know that, at least, they can go somewhere and check up on that process.

Guarding this kind of information is a practice that is dead. Today's sellers demand partnerships with their agents. You must rise to this challenge, or face the prospect of complaining clients...

In fact, the top three seller complaints are ALL related to poor communication:

- *The agent doesn't return phone calls.*
- *The agent doesn't call unless we call first.*
- *We don't know what the agent is doing to sell our property.*

Remember: bad communication is the biggest contributor to low productivity and negative client relationships.

Sellers don't care if it's time-consuming – they expect good, consistent communication from their agents! For instance, email is an effective, low-cost and trackable way to keep in touch with clients and prospects. Below we will look at how you can automate this communication tool to better serve you – and your clients.

Negative Communication

Your crankiest customers are broadcasting to the world! And, nowadays, word of mouth isn't limited to their closest acquaintances... Real estate agent rating sites are proliferating on the internet, making it fast and easy for unhappy clients to share their complaints with potential customers in your area (and around the globe!). Zillow.com now offers agent ratings and sites like www.agentratingz.com allow consumers to rate their REALTOR®.

Of course, there are also Twitter, Facebook, Yelp.com, blogs, and an onslaught of other social media avenues for broadcasting complaints to a huge audience today. Inevitably, these online complaints mirror these top three seller complaints. For instance, here are several real complaints from a real estate agent rating site:

> *"This real estate agent was extremely unresponsive and would take weeks to return calls and emails. We decided to move on to someone more efficient and knowledgeable."*

> *"Agent failed to communicate while house was on the market. Waited until the market fell so bad in my area, I was unable to sell. He never called to let us know the market conditions, failed to communicate weekly..."*

Similarly, sellers who don't hear from you on a frequent basis will speak out:

> *"Did not answer emails or phone calls, or text messages."*

> *"...does not provide updates even when requested and avoids phone calls...It takes her several days (or never) to return calls."*

> *"In today's market, communication and customer service skills are key to keeping clients. I am moving on to another REALTOR®... not because my house hasn't sold, but because I do not feel the quality of service I desire is present."* (Source: http://www.realestateratingz.com)

Research shows that people will tell others about negative experiences two to three times more often than they'll mention a positive experience. While a happy customer will tell no more than five people – if that – on average, an unhappy customer will tell 15 people! Then those 15 people will tell five more each... and the poison pool spreads, getting worse in the telling. (*Source: How damaging is negative word of mouth? – Marketing Bulletin, 1995*)

Therefore, if a client is particularly unhappy with your service, you will lose not just the current listing, but future ones. We have seen that 18% of buyers and 26% of sellers will use agents they have used before. Multiple studies have shown that it costs 5 to10 times more money to replace lost customers than to retain current customers. (*Source: Profit Brand, by Nick Wreden*)

Furthermore, over a half of the 3,500+ consumer respondents in an Accenture survey reported their expectations for better service have increased over the past five years. A majority of consumers reported that they had quit doing business with a company due to poor service.

The bottom line is: clients will leave for your competition if they aren't treated well, so pay close attention to every aspect of communication and strive to foster positive relationships with these walking, talking advertisements.

 Frequency of Communication

How often is often? And how often isn't often enough? We recommend Alan Shafran's frequency grading system to make certain that you're communicating in an effective and time-conscious manner.

It's easy as **ABC123** – this grading method involves categorizing clients based upon their perceived motivation and chance of success. The minute they walk through the door, talk to you on the phone or you have their information from your website, you need to evaluate a potential client. Based on that evaluation, you can decide how best to spend your time and energies.

Here's how it breaks down:

- *'A' clients are eager to sell or buy quickly, with over 90% chance they are going to complete the transaction.*
- *'B' clients seem enthusiastic and interested, with between 50 and 90% chance of closing the deal.*
- *'C' clients are requesting information, but appear not to be motivated to move quickly like the 'A's and 'B's, so they are considered less than a 50% chance of going through.*

As a result of these simple classifications, the 'A' clients are treated with a higher priority than clients lower down the food chain.

This method is based on the daily decision we have to make as agents where, if the phones started ringing and everyone called in at the same time, you'd have to make a choice about who is your top priority. Although it may sound harsh, it's actually about focusing on the right clients so that they receive the right frequency of communication, and ultimately ensuring the success of your business.

Often we will take clients with a certain direction or understanding that they're a minimum of a 'B' client. Naturally, the situation may change for them and they might not be as interested as before, so they can be moved to a 'C', and some 'C's turn into 'B's and even an 'A.' We're constantly reevaluating the situation and using our best judgment to assess the sales leads coming into our office.

Once we know whether the client is an A, B or C, then we apply the numbers 1, 2, or 3. This relates to how often we contact the client, per week. Our goal is over-servicing. Ideally, we want the client to say that we're talking to them too much, too often.

For instance, with the 'A' clients, they always start at a 3 – we would call them 3 times a week; Monday, Wednesday, Friday. They sometimes tell us to call them just once a week, but we begin with an 'A3' to get the ball rolling and assess their desire for frequent communication. Consequently, you never want a client to call in and say, *"I've been waiting for a phone call…"*

It's worth noting that it would be rare to have a 'C' client who receives more than 1 call per week. A typical client list may look like this: A3, A2, B2, B1, C1, C1… And, once again, you're always assessing and evaluating the changes in their needs or the perceived chance of success, then moving the clients through the appropriate categories of ABC123. In addition, a technology like ShowingSuite.com, also contributes effortless yet timely communication with the sellers above and beyond the ABC123 system. All of a sudden, your service to your customer makes you a superstar!

Of course, every client is different – there are clients who prefer to receive phone call updates and there are others who prefer text messages or emails. The key is having a business that's flexible enough to make as many clients as happy as possible; that's the way that you build a good repeat and referral business.

Remember, referrals are a huge source of clients – we have seen that 43% of buyers and 38% of sellers choose their agents through referrals. *(Source: National Association of REALTORS® Profile of Home buyers and sellers, 2007-2008)*

Team Communication
When establishing an ABC123 system, it's equally important that the whole team is apprised of which clients fall under which category. The team needs to be synchronized and on the same page, otherwise an 'A' client might fall through the cracks and not receive the proper attention that is deserved, or a 'C' client might fall right off the radar entirely.

Also, bad communication can undercut agent morale, so it's critical to hold weekly Team Meetings and Team Training. In these sessions, agents should be told what we're dealing with in today's marketplace, and there should be constant review of scripts and systems. It's tedious and difficult, but this is the secret to the success of a sales team.

 Technology

All contact information including grading and communication should be kept in a shared CRM (Customer Relationship Management) cloud based software and updated after every contact. Here, all team members can share contacts and the system is available inside the office, form the agents home computers, and via their mobile devices. ShowingSuite.com is an example of this service with their team version for contact and listing sharing.

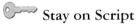 Stay on Script

Sales scripts are a huge part of the communication that occurs in the real estate biz. These are tried and tested dialogues that lead to completed transactions.

The right script, said the right way, is key to the sales side of the business. Agents on your team need to know these scripts and rigidly follow them; you can't just say whatever you want, any way you want. The training and context is critical.

In our team meetings and training, we focus on a lot of role-playing, going over scripts and what to say in certain situations. We make the agents memorize the script, then role play and practice it. This attention to detail improves the overall communication between the team, and communication with the clients who will essentially be playing an actual role in this script in a real life scenario. Schedule a minimum of biweekly meetings for script role playing. A sample scripts schedule:

- *First & Third Monday each month 8:30 – 9:20 buyer rep call scripts*
- *First & Third Tuesdays 9:30 – 10:20 FSBO call scripts*
- *Second & Fourth Wednesday 8:30 – 9:20 buyer listing scripts*
- *Second & Fourth Thursday 9:30 – 10:20 seller listing scripts*

Coop Agent Communication

Most often, there will be two agents in the transaction – you and the other guy. The old joke we use when we represent both sides of the transaction is that we love communicating with the buyer's agent. Of course, communication is a two-way street, yet there is a huge number of REALTORS® typically in every city, and everyone has a different type of attitude about how to approach coop agents. Some like to over-service them. For example, ShowingSuite.com builds for you a database of all the Showing Agents who have shown your listings and easily contacts them about homes they have shown or new listings that you have.

We think that this relationship is important and we are willing to use a tool such as Showing Suite to manage that process and service these coop agents, without having it bore into our time for our assistants or ourselves as much as possible.

Nevertheless, say I've got a listing and I treat the coop agent in a friendly and open manner, so we're on a professional level. Of course, not every time will the other agent be cordial – some are antagonistic, they can have an attitude, or be aloof. Although, once they know how you conduct yourself and how you handle the business, they know you're real and your clients are real, and you have a better chance of closing a deal – one that won't fall apart – all because you are communicating this style and philosophy to them.

If you build your reputation in the real estate community, it will serve your interests. For instance, if there are 3 offers on the table – one from me, one from a stranger, and one from a REALTOR® who they've had a bad experience with – we might not have the best price on this occasion, but the agent will come back to us first, as he would rather be working with us. They will explain to their seller that they don't know the other agents, but they do know that if a member of Alan's team brings an offer it is likely more solid than the others and has a higher chance of closing. Also, many times, they will bring us a counter offer first, rather than send multiple offers out, in the hopes they can get their price from the strongest buyer's agent who can get the escrow closed. Negotiations in multiple counter offers are very tricky and sensitive. There are a plethora of different strategies that both sides of the table can use. The truth is that a whole book can be written on negotiation in our business and that will be forthcoming from us as well in our next book.

That's the reality, especially when there are multiple offers. You need to pick a deal which will close at the end of the day, so agents will be evaluating you and categorizing you in the same vein of the ABC123 system.

Therefore, who the agent is definitely plays a part in the equation when making a real estate deal.

Capture Leads and Nurture Them

Of course, communication isn't just about how you conduct yourself with current contacts; it's also about nurturing new leads.

With the majority of people using the Internet to begin their housing research today, it is imperative to capture and follow up on Internet leads. Did you know that 19 out of 20 online leads are from consumers who are still in the information-gathering stage of house-hunting, and may be three to six months away from moving to the active phase? *(Source: REALTOR® Magazine Online, 5/1/2007)*

Regardless, they can be converted to active clients, but only by first capturing their information and then nurturing the relationship.

See Chapter 6 for Lead Nurturing technology.

 ## Building a Brand

Who are *you*? You want the prospects that you capture, and target, to remember your name. The goal of branding is to make your practice or agency synonymous with the best in real estate services. More than 1/3 of sellers say reputation is the most critical factor in choosing an agent. *(Source: National Association of REALTORS® Profile of Home buyers and sellers, 2007-2008)*

Think about what you are communicating in your 'brand'. To build your profile and branding, all of your communication to your clients and prospects should portray a consistent image and a consistent look and feel. Always think carefully about how you convey your brand and how to set your practice apart in what you offer your clients – but also set yourself on a whole different playing field above your competition.

FYI – Real estate professionals need to touch their market at least 18 times per year to forge a solid memory, so people opt to call you when they are ready to buy or sell. This means constant communication with them.

Thus, you could try this: when a prospect signs up for a newsletter on your website, the data they input automatically kicks off the marketing process. They will be sent the newsletter throughout the year, along with any other communications you have programmed as appropriate... Time passes, but your name continually stays in front of that prospect as they receive your frequent correspondence. Then, when they decide to sell their house, the REALTOR® they will automatically think of is you!

Ultimately, you want to be known in your market, and this is all about how you're communicating and personifying your attitude to clients, prospects, and other agents who cross paths with you. Never forget it.

See Chapter 5 for automated follow-up technology and conversion secrets.

🔑 Home Feedback

This is one of the main points of interaction between you and a coop agent, and eventually the client. It can be a bone of contention, and sellers will expect feedback no matter what, so it's very important.

However, it's not always easy to get sellers the information they crave, or address the buyers' concerns in order to quickly sell their house. Typically, listing agents spin their wheels with repeated time-intensive phone calls and emails, only to get a paltry 20% response rate – that's 80% of your time wasted! And just as important, an 80% failure rate in the seller's eyes.

Could you pay an assistant to chase feedback? Sure, but then 80% of your money is wasted. And besides, only 14% of REALTORS® have a personal assistant. *(Source: REALTOR® Magazine Online, National Association of REALTORS®)*

Hint – For transparency, have a seller portal that sellers can login to 24/7 and view their showing and feedback information. Also set up email templates to automatically fire off personalized feedback requests – and do so three times or more until the showing agent responds.

Make sure the emails are written in a cooperative manner and that the feedback you are requesting has questions that are specifically related to that one property. You also want photos of the property that they had shown to remind them which showing you are requesting feedback about.

Also, ensure you use email templates branded with your look and feel – with every communication you are also marketing to showing agents!

Many independent agents don't bother responding to coop agent's inquiries at all, or in a very slow fashion at the least. Tracking down showing agents is time-consuming and thankless. In order to get feedback to the seller, a listing agent traditionally has to:

- *Call and email, repeatedly.*
- *Transcribe comments into a professional-looking report.*
- *Deliver the report to the sellers – who may not like or believe the feedback they see!*

Why does HomeFeedback.com succeed?? It is one of the few companies that was able to successfully fill in the hole of communication between several parties, leveraging the use of the internet since 2001. Just as important, the company understands the roles of the agent clearly along with the desires of the consumer. As one of the industries revolutionizing technologies, HomeFeedback.com is making regular improvements to allow the agent to receive the credit for the service vs. the technology. In addition, the company is constantly striving to add constant flexibility to the economic and industry's latest changes. For example, the latest change will be in the rare case that an agent does not respond to 3 feedback attempts. After the 3rd failed attempt (less than 20% of the time), HomeFeedback.com will send an email to the agent giving them the option to send the standard response to the seller, customize the response, call the seller from a button in the email, along with several other options. HomeFeedback.com has serviced hundreds of thousands of real estate agents nationally and internationally. The company learned early on that in order for technology to succeed for the agents, it must have an organic type of software that grows and adapts to the agents' and consumers' needs. This is the kind of technology we recommend that you adapt in your business in every segment you can possibly find. Although they are not always easy to find, when you finally do, your business world will change in a massive positive direction both fiscally and personally.

This leads us to dealing with the client's expectations of the feedback...

Client's Expectations
What do clients expect from feedback? Quite often, they expect sunshine and happiness. After all – they love their home, why shouldn't someone else?!

Unfortunately, when sellers do get negative feedback on their home and particularly the price, they often won't listen. Even with the bad news all over the TV and newspapers, many home owners still don't get it when it comes to setting realistic prices for their properties.

Take this into consideration:

- *75% of agents surveyed report that most sellers have unrealistic initial listing prices for their homes.*
- *In 2008, as real estate prices plummeted, 62% of home owners thought their home's price had increased or stayed the same during the past year. (Source: Columbus Dispatch, 11/16/2008)*

As a result of these unreal expectations, many sellers may refuse to lower their prices, then decide the reason their house won't move is because they have an incompetent agent – and that's what they tell all their friends and coworkers!

Ultimately, sellers in deep denial eat into your earnings and your time. Some sellers are so deeply in denial about setting a realistic price for their home that agents would rather walk away from the listing than spend time and money on a drawn-out selling effort.

Anything you can do to bring starry-eyed sellers down to earth is going to translate into improving your bottom line. A great way is using the showing statistics tool, like in Showing Suite. When sellers see a stat such as 79% of all agents who have provided feedback said their home was "above market value," it starts the process of getting realistic expectations on the table. Sellers will even ask you to reduce the listing price when you set up an effective and transparent process like Showing Suite's Home Feedback tool.

Getting <u>REAL</u> Real Estate Feedback
Another big problem with real estate feedback is that it's not always genuine. When listing agents do give feedback, they often paint too rosy a picture. They don't want to hurt the sellers' feelings. They mince their words and skirt around the truth, which is less helpful than getting zero feedback.

Nevertheless, interrogating the agents doesn't improve the quality of the feedback. What we have found with Home Feedback is that, rather than holding the agents accountable for feedback, which they found threatening, instead it helps to encourage a cooperative relationship. By letting the other agent know that if they provide feedback on this listing for you and your seller, then you will do the same when you show one of their listings; this reciprocal practice helps to make feedback a more accepted system in the coop community. You will provide feedback on their listings, if they will do the same for yours. Everyone's back gets scratched in this equation.

Automating Feedback
Through use of a tool like Showing Suite's HomeFeedback.com, we've seen expedited responses and service, the right kind of inquiry on a listing, and we've built rapports between agents, and helped motivate clients to move on a particular home, simply because it's represented better. They know that when a REALTOR® has everything together, the disclosures will be right, too. Basically, you are communicating that you are at a first-class level of competence and professionalism.

In our opinion, to save time and money, a feedback request should be triggered automatically:

- *When showing agents calendar a showing of the house on your website, your sellers should be sent an email.*
- *When a showing agent uses a lock box to access the house, that information should be fed back to the system so that, within an hour or so, the showing agent automatically receives an email request for feedback that includes multiple photos, questions of your choosing, and a link so he can reach the feedback form quickly and easily.*

This way, sellers know what's going on immediately. Sellers, alerted by an email, can read this feedback on your website in real time, as well as reports that give them percentages of how people answered the questions. And if showing agents don't respond after multiple automatic requests, sellers are alerted to that, too.

Ultimately, sellers are in the loop, via an online portal, where they can view all of their showing activity, feedback provided, feedback statistics and feedback gathering status. This way, the feedback process is completely transparent.

In terms of response rates, emails seeking feedback that are sent automatically to showing agents raise these responses from 20% to over 70%. When showing agents don't respond, a follow-up email can be sent automatically stating, *"We tried on 3 occasions to get the feedback from Jane Agent. We were unsuccessful, but we will continue our marketing efforts with your home."* Now the seller knows it wasn't your fault you didn't get the feedback; it was the showing agent who refused to provide it. Now compare that versus telling a $600k seller that you tried to call the showing agent three times, but he wouldn't return the calls. Who is to blame in this scenario?

And, on the same feedback website, sellers can also see the marketing you have been doing. This shared information creates a partnership between you and the seller that removes the need for you to pressure them to make needed repairs or change pricing.

As a result of this automation, the technology takes the **blame** off you, the agent, by confirming to the seller that you are doing your job to the best of your ability. It also takes some of the responsibilities off of your shoulders – it takes tens of hours a month, chasing, gathering and communicating feedback…

If you have 25 or more listings, that means you probably need a full-time admin assistant to handle feedback and answer to the seller (and answer to the seller's high expectations for prompt and detailed comments), which is why it makes sense to have an automated system in place such as ShowingSuite.com.

Client Satisfaction

The final part of the communication process is surveying your clients at the end of a transaction. This provides valuable information about how to improve your business and the communication links between agents and customers.

Once again, this can be automated and coordinated via email. Consider asking your clients, *"How would you rate our communication skills?"* 1=Great, 5= Terrible. You will be surprised at how honest, and potentially helpful, their responses are.

There are technologies to set up to send satisfaction surveys such as surveymonkey. com, zoomerang.com or a real estate specific one like ShowingSuite.com.

Conclusion

Excellent communication between your team and your clients, both buyers and sellers, is the foundation upon which your real estate practice will rise or fall! If communicating smartly and cohesively, you will be able to:

- *Focus on your best prospects*
- *Deliver necessary and valuable feedback*
- *Coordinate effectively with other agents*
- *Synchronize and improve your team*
- *Market with precision*
- *Put systems in place to fast-track the process of getting in touch with every one of your past clients regularly throughout the year*
- *Create referral reward programs for your clients*
- *Implement regular email campaigns that give your clients valuable information — not just blatant sales pitches*
- *Automate your home feedback process providing a seller transparency portal*
- *Know your market segments, and match your messages accordingly.*

- *Fine-tune and aggressively promote what makes your agency different and better.*

Continuing some of the Communication concepts mentioned in this chapter, next we will focus more closely on Marketing methods...

Read on... Chapter 5: Social and Not so Social Marketing

Chapter 5
Social (& Not So Social) Marketing

The marketing tools available to REALTORS® have changed considerably since the early days of door-knocking, open houses, sending out flyers, even delivering pumpkins in October. We're now in the era of Web 2.0 and beyond, with internet and social marketing tools, which are more cost-and-time-effective than anything that we've ever tried before.

As long as you're using them in the right way, and efficiently, there are many advantages to blogs, Facebook, Twitter, and other websites for connecting with your consumers.

Social Marketing
Consider the story of Gary Vaynerchuck, who is now renowned as a pioneer in social media, promoting his wine-tasting reviews website (www.winelibrarytv. com) via Twitter and Facebook, as well as Vlogs (video blogs), turning it into an overnight sensation. He now gives keynote presentations and consults Fortune 500 companies on this technique, which caught the eye of the business world and is recognized as a thought-leading approach to savvy and skilful marketing for the 21st Century.

Vaynerchuck realized early on, as did we in the real estate business – you need to go where your prospects are. And this means going online.

Of course, many of these blogging and tweeting sites might sound like a 'waste of time' and a sure-fire way to burn hundreds of man-hours surfing and posting new articles and information. *How can these sites bring in leads? How do I stay on top of these technological developments, without getting bogged down with spending all day in front of a computer? Is this really a worthwhile use of my energies?*

The answer is yes, this is worthwhile. But, the key is automation, automation, and then automating your automation. First, you must understand the process and put your personality, character, and personal touch into your systems. Then, you need to set-up the appropriate 'nets' to bring in the prospects, and from there — if you're getting enough prospects — you will certainly need to automate the process, or you will be very busy; too busy to handle the incoming leads and close these deals.

Fishing for Sellers with Tech Lures

When 'fishing' in the open waters of real estate, the trick is to have a multitude of sources and thus having many poles in the water. We don't know if having the biggest net in a single place really works, but we do know that having a decent-sized net in many well placed spots is most practical and productive.

Your lead goal is to get conversions and initially, that means catching a fresh lead — and by this, we mean a real lead. It was more common in the past to get a time-waster who provides a bogus phone number, or a bogus email address. However, nowadays, in the age of Spam, those who understand the web wouldn't even bother including a number or email address if they weren't serious about receiving a reply.

As in fishing, it is not easy to know where the fish are unless you know the waters, conditions and what will make the fish strike at your bait. Unfortunately, there isn't a single answer or specific route to recommend in the practice of fishing. What might work for us, won't necessarily work in a different market with different customers. However, the one thing that does work is testing, testing, and testing. There are fish, so if you test those waters over and over, eventually you will find a place where they're biting and how to make them strike...

Of course, we need to bear in mind that, just because it works today, there are no guarantees that the customers will be there a month from now, or that a competitor won't figure out the same idea. There's a reason it's called "fishing" and not "catching." You need to keep on top of the market conditions, which market is moving in real estate and what motivates these folks to contact you.

And once you've tested the waters and found something that works or doesn't work, then it's time to tweak that testing.

We recommend that you read up on A/B split testing to zero in on the single variable that is most effective. Also, you should look into using free analytics tools for your website to see where your prospects are dropping off, where your traffic is coming from, what are your popular site pages, etc... We like Google Analytics for this service www.google.com/analytics and it's free.

Another example is how the auto industry has adapted to the tech change regarding prospective buyers. The auto dealers understand there are two primary different types of buyers; online and onsite. Onsite are traditional buyers that need to see, feel, and touch the product and the sales process. These buyers walk onto the dealership, test drive the car several times, look for a rapport with their sales person, and enjoy surviving the negotiation process. In turn, the dealership takes them through the appropriate sales process including what might be a painful negotiation process.

Conversely, the auto dealers understand the online buyer, too. This buyer isn't interested in a conversation with the auto dealer, sales person, etc. Several years ago, the auto dealers still tried onsite tactics with the online buyer; today, they realize this is a lost cause. Now the auto dealers assign a special online representative who is an expert at this style of communication. This online representative's goal is to respond as fast as possible and with a no haggle, no hassle price and buying process. This communicates trust to the online buyer. In addition, the online representative understands that he may only have one shot at gaining the buyer's confidence or the buyer is off to the next online dealership.

The question for you is: *Do you have flexible sales systems that can accommodate a multitude of customers, especially the online customer?*

We've been doing our testing for quite some time. In the beginning, we started with a service where we loaded diskettes; the software automatically dialed a data phone number at night, and connected over a modem to send updates and new listings... Back then, 12 years ago, we were at the forefront of the technology side of this business, and we strive to remain at the cutting edge today so we can get to the fish before anyone else.

Without a doubt, we've come a long way from door-to-door pumpkins, too; those were the old days of marketing, prior to the personal computer and advent of the Internet. And since the Internet was created, the number of possible sources for leads has grown exponentially over the years. *What lures will you test to catch the most?*

 Fishing for Buyers with IDX

The main source of buyers can be through a real estate property search website, which involves an Internet Data Exchange, or IDX. Internet users want control with transparency to data and IDX provides this. This allows prospects to search for themselves, with homes streaming automatically from a Multiple Listing Service data feed. This searching can be anonymous, or they may be required to register their information with the IDX website.

You can test different ways to capture the data of those surfing the IDX. But, the trick is to capture leads from it. The best way to do this is give away the service for free and then to turn these browsers into buyers… We were the first in San Diego that started with the concept of IDX websites, offering different search systems and giving this information to buyers, essentially so they would give us their data in return.

These were the original 'Stealth' sites (long before the term 'Stealth' was ever used in this way) and we developed these sites to appear autonomous from our own enterprises. Therefore, instead of coming to a site named *RickBengson.com* or *AlanShafran.com*, if you wanted to see available homes in the year 2000 in San Diego, you visited our sites: *FreeSanDiegoHomeSearch.com* or *SDHomeFinder.com*.

We created these independent brands that are apparently unrelated to our real estate business. Yet, they were incredibly bountiful for generating leads!

Many users couldn't differentiate between our sites and *REALTOR.com* – other agents were even framing our free website into theirs. As a result, their clients were actually registering on our site! What is our point? Think like the customer, not like a REALTOR®.

How are our consumers getting to us today? What gives them the confidence to use us? How do they find us? You must truly think outside of the box and be willing to change your systems often, as that is the reality of the times that we live in.

What we did with our stealth sites was start fishing at a time when the only net was the Internet itself. But, this was also about testing the terrain, and we learned some tips to consider when seeking an IDX provider for your website:

- *Find an IDX provider that will give you **flexibility** – some will ask users to register before they can even look at a property, or will specify how many anonymous searches they can do before going any further (e.g. 3 searches then you need to register as a user). The more options you have, the better testing you can perform.*
- *Find an IDX provider that will give you **user transparency** – where you can see what users are searching, then set up a system – not just to keep track of these leads, but keep in contact with them, too.*
- *It can also be helpful to see what your prospects are searching for so when you contact them you can have a property ready to discuss that fits their particular needs.*
- *There are even IDX sites today which customize to the needs and wants of the individual customer and adapt the searches accordingly.*

Remember, this is all about making technology work for us, so we don't have to do all the hard work. After your IDX is successfully working prospects will be receiving property updates automatically and raise their hands when they need help from you. You can set it to focus on high end buyers or first time home buyers, investors etc. Find an IDX that will take care of the heavy lifting for you, learn it well, and test it thoroughly for the best prospect catches for your business...

Branding

As we've discussed earlier in the book, how you brand yourself, your business, and your website will make a big difference to your degree of success – especially when attracting the big fish or a large school of fish.

You want the prospects that you target to remember your name and ultimately your brand will help to build your credibility and the desire to work with your team. Thus, the goal of branding is to make your online presence, and your agency, synonymous with the quality of the real estate services that you represent.

The brand should, naturally, speak to your customer. There are a few different types of customers that you may choose to target and it becomes expensive and inefficient to market to all of them. Therefore, it makes good business sense to become a specialist in your niche and focus all of your marketing and branding in that arena.

To build your brand, all of your communications to your clients and prospects should portray a consistent image and a consistent look and feel.

Think carefully about how you can not only set your practice apart in what you offer your clients, but also set yourself on a whole different playing field above your competition.

Branding to consider:

- *Logo – design or select an image that personifies your style and quality. Spend money on professional graphics and don't use your headshot no matter how good you look.*
- *Website – build a site that reflects the brand and sets you apart from other REALTORS® in your region.*
- *Interactive – you may want a personalized video about you and your team, or describing your specialty.*

Speed to Lead

Rick says: *"When I first started out, I thought, 'When I get a lead, I don't want to jump all over them... Instead, I'll give them a couple of days, then call them. I don't want to come across as too eager, so I will give them some space.' This is absolutely the wrong thing to do.*

Over 50% of internet real estate shoppers do not have an agent and, of those who buy, over 95% will end up using an agent. You want to get to them before they get to another real estate website and that agent contacts them, instills confidence with them and subsequently gets their business.

Because, ultimately, what you're after are prospects that aren't referred to an agent and you must get to them before the other 300 or 3500 members of your MLS do... They don't have an allegiance to anybody. That 50% of the leads out there are without a sphere of influence and open to working with you.

Simply, you can't call these people fast enough – and when you call them quickly, you will hear their appreciation: 'Wow that was fast, you're on the ball' – This is why I always say 'Speed to Lead.'

When I started SDHomeFinder.com, one of the very first leads that I received was a buyer prospect lead looking for a 'minimum of 1 bedroom, up to $1 million' – this was in 1999, and I thought it was the goofiest lead I'd ever heard of. Of course you would get more than 1 bedroom for $1 million!? Putting this feeling aside, I called the prospect and sold them a house that week for $930,000. The client even told me the exact house he wanted to see as it was advertised in the paper that day...

The first one to make contact wins. If I hadn't called right away, I would've missed out on a $28,000 commission."

⚷ Thus, our recommendation is: where humanly possible – call, email, SMS... whatever. Contact the new leads within an hour. Preferably within 5 minutes. By doing so, assuming that you're presenting yourself properly and professionally, there's no reason why you won't make the first impression – and the best impression – to convert that lead into a client.

⚷ Conversion Secrets

When aiming for 100 deals, the key is converting as many leads as possible. This means attracting quality leads, and reacting quickly when a new lead arises, but it also helps if you have a solid grasp of who your customers are and the market in your area.

- *Put yourself in the consumer's shoes* – *Understand their experiences and see the world from their point of view.*
- *Build your website accordingly* – *Style your site around that customer experience that you want to deliver to the consumer.*
- *Keep it simple* – *Don't overload them with information; attract them in, be useful, and then close the deal.*
- *Build confidence* – *explain your local market knowledge or your new home construction expertise or whatever you have in your arsenal to let that prospect know you are bringing something to the table that they can't just find over the internet and they should be helped by someone like you.*
- *Be reachable, personable, and prompt* – *When the 'hand raisers' approach you, don't let them slip through the net.*
- *Show Value and express quickly why the consumer should contact you NOW!*
- *Close for an appointment* – *You will need an appointment to represent them as their agent. Seal the deal and get the client.*

Nevertheless, the number one secret is, as we've mentioned before, **automation**. It's critically important that your business has automated systems – unless you already have the infrastructure of a large team in place to cope with the incoming leads that your nets will yield.

Essentially, you either need a team to manage all of these leads, or a systematic plan to manage them automatically without putting pressure on yourself or your admin team.

For example, it's possible to put all of your incoming leads into a 'drip' email campaign, which will send out an email on Day 1, 2, 3, 5, 7, 12... These emails should appear to be personal, like they were written by an actual agent, not just a computer-generated stock newsletter. Then, we wait for someone to respond, and that would be the <u>hot</u> lead you need to contact. This is one who has raised their hand that they need help, and you need to pounce on that one as soon as possible.

It helps if you use a real estate specific email campaign manager like www.HomeFollowup.com that can integrate with your website. This way, your campaigns start immediately after the prospect signs up from the form on your website and you don't have to copy and paste emailed data. Basically, you don't have to reinvent the wheel. Think about how many times you started a project that you couldn't finish. Execution is the majority of success, so just pick a system that has been proven to work and go, go, go! Automate the process.

Email Do's and Don'ts

Email is effective and low cost, as proven by a recent survey of agents which showed that email campaigns, as opposed to direct mail campaigns, are:

Faster and easier: 42%

Less expensive: 26%

More professional looking: 16%

Generate higher response rates: 12%

(Source: Businesswire.com)

Another benefit is that you can precisely track online marketing. With today's technology, you can see exactly the number of email messages sent, which messages were undeliverable, which messages were opened, how many links were clicked... etc.

By testing with hard data like that, you no longer have to guess whether your marketing efforts were worth the time and money.

According to an Email Marketing Metrics Report (November 2008), a high percentage of people open email from real estate agents. Compared to other direct marketing vehicles, email produces the highest absolute response rates for generating leads:

Real Estate marketing emails generate one of the highest "open rates" among all industries: 17.74%
The news is even better for click-through rates for included links: Average: 2.73%, Real Estate: 7%

Make it Personal

As we've mentioned, it helps to make the email appear like it's coming directly from you, and not some machine. Research shows that just adding a client or prospect's name to an email more than doubles open rates and increases click-through rates by 60%! Use an email signature that is branded to yourself or your team with consistency across the team to look professional.

And yet...

75% of companies do not personalize their email!

85% fail to personalize the first message!

60% fail to send a welcome message to new subscribers to newsletters or other information offers!

(Source: Email Marketing Metrics Report, November 2008)

More Links = More Click-through

Emails with over 20 links are more than twice as likely to have higher click-through rates as emails with five. Below are general figures. (We have seen industry click-through rates are higher):

1-5 links: 1.72% clicks

6-10 links: 1.39% clicks

11-20 links: 2.26% clicks

20+ links: 3.51% clicks

Therefore, don't be afraid to include a lot of links in your email – even if some of them take the reader to the same place!

Length and Timing Matter

Emails sent Sunday through Tuesday have the highest open rate. Click rates are steady across all days of the weeks.

Also, bear in mind that shorter subject lines are better.

Open rates for marketing email overall:
> *<35 characters: 19.64%*

> *>35 characters: 14.83%*

> *(25% increase for shorter subject lines)*

Click rates (general figures):

> *<35 characters: 3.05%*

> *>35 characters: 1.93%*

> *(37% difference favoring short subject lines)*

> *(Source: Email Marketing Metrics Report, November 2008)*

Track Everything

If you track all of these efforts, then you can focus your marketing on what is most effective. We recommend an automated system that provides real-time reporting and enables you to see which of your marketing activities are generating the most leads.

By knowing where the leads are actually coming from, this data makes it easy to target marketing efforts in the future that maximize responses for each client segment.

Heed Federal Law

Just a word of caution – The Federal CAN-SPAM Act of 2003 requires that all commercial email:

- *Include a valid return address*
- *A method to opt out*
- *Include the sender's valid physical address and contact information*

Put systems in place to be sure these rules are adhered to and that any email you send is viewed as informational and valuable – not Spam.

Today, software is available with templates that take care of this for you.

Because of Spam emails, your legitimate emails could potentially get caught in a filter. Ask your prospects to place your email address on a 'White List' to stop yourself getting relegated with the rest of the Spam!

Did you know…?

- *90% of incoming email is Spam, so many ISPs block or blacklist email coming from some addresses.*
- *Spam filters successfully catch an estimated 90 to 99% of the remaining Spam.*
- *Unfortunately, Spam filters also stop delivery of 1% to 10% of legitimate email.*
- *Legitimate emails that are erroneously blocked costs marketers $107 million yearly.*
  (Source: Spamhaus.org, Emaillabs.com, NetSecurity.org)

To keep your email from getting caught in Spam filters, here are some extra steps you can take:

- *Verify compliance with the 21 pages of provisions in the Federal CAN-SPAM Act of 2003.*
- *Stay in contact with major ISPs and Spam filter companies to ensure that you're not erroneously blacklisted.*
- *Scrupulously edit every message to avoid dangerous words and phrases that trigger Spam filters.*
  (Source: Federal Trade Commission)

Another option is to find a technology provider who will do all this for you while you concentrate on real estate.

When choosing a technology provider to automate your email and online marketing, make certain that they are:

- *Partnered with a legitimate reputation service provider that;*
- *Certifies compliance with federal regulations;*

- *Maintains relationships with major ISPs to ensure white-listing of IP numbers and email addresses;*
- *And notifies the technology provider if blacklisting occurs so the technology provider can take steps to remove you from the blacklist.*

Also be certain that your technology provider:

- *Protects your messages from being blocked by ISPs by avoiding sending too many messages too fast.*
- *Sends each email as a "solo" message so ISPs don't mistake it for Spam.*
- *Provides pre-created campaigns that have been checked for problem phrases to avoid words and phrases that trigger Spam filters.*
- *Has multiple full-time Spam officers on staff whose sole responsibilities are monitoring blacklists and handling any issues that may arise.*

See Chapter 6 for systems technology to do this for you.

The Ratio of Leads to Conversions?

With all your nets set, and emails sent, you're probably wondering how many leads it will take to reach a goal of 100 deals…

> Alan says: *"I will typically receive 300 leads per week. That number also fluctuates up and down with economic climate, of course. Referrals are 30-40% of my business, and even then I am prospecting for those referrals, contacting past clients to keep up with them…*
>
> *The remaining leads are generated by marketing systems. Out of these, every 20 leads = 1 conversion.*
>
> *This ratio used to be much higher; the truth is, many more people feel more comfortable using the internet for communication and searching, and those who aren't serious don't want to be contacted, so they don't supply contact info. As a result, we get less leads, but the quality of the leads has definitely gone up…"*

Capture Leads and Nurture Them

With the majority of people using the Internet to begin their housing research today, we cannot stress enough how it is imperative to capture and follow up on these leads, to nurture them into conversions, and ultimately add to your 100 deals total for the year.

Remember – 19 out of 20 online leads are from consumers who are still in the information-gathering stage of house-hunting and may be three to six months away from moving to the active phase. *(Source: REALTOR® Magazine Online, 5/1/2007)*

They can be converted to active clients, but only by first capturing their information and then nurturing the relationship.

Marketing Organically

As marketers of our business, we always have to decide where to spend our money, in order to best deliver results.

This is why it's crucial to examine the 'organic' methods of marketing on the internet – these are the unpaid results derived from blogs and raising your profile on 'free' social marketing sites like Facebook. Moreover, through search engine optimization (SEO), the text on your sites and the way your site is optimized can generate more traffic without you paying a cent.

Of course, organic – if done properly – can be expensive in the beginning (the architecture of the website and its content need to be created), but more cost effective in the end. Expect to take 12-24 months in the development of your organic system to see real results; this is the investment that is needed, and mostly it will cost you time.

If you're considering a blog, then remember that search engines like Google prefer content that's changing regularly, it also likes videos, and sites linking to you, and streaming RSS feeds...

By the way, if all this tech-speak brings out the technophobe in you, then it's probably a good idea to turn to someone on your team who will coordinate these efforts. It's important to have team members that specialize in the website and marketing services. Don't worry if you feel daunted – there are REALTORS® who have been doing over 100 deals a year, and they don't even know how to use email (someone else does it for them).

Bottom line – good business people are aware of what they're good at, and how to best use their time to make money, then they delegate the rest. There are REALTORS® who don't have a clue about tech and they risk falling into a black hole if they endeavor to learn it all, instead of keeping their focus on the real estate side of the business.

Regardless, for REALTORS® in the future, these organic marketing techniques are a better way to go in the long-run, from a financial perspective.

🔑 Paid Search aka PPC (Pay-Per-Click)

This is what makes Google the multi-billion-dollar juggernaut it is today. PPC are the paid advertisements when you perform a keyword search on a search engine. These ads are typically on the top of the page along with the right hand column. It is a great way to get immediate traffic to your website, but you have to pay for it. When building your business and your fishing website, 'Pay-Per-Click' online advertising may be appropriate for quickly solidifying your reputation and targeting surfers in your geographic area. A free way to learn how PPC works and strategies along with opening an account is Google Adwords www.google.com/adwords.

Whatever you're currently doing for advertising, basically you need to shift it over to the internet. Eventually, close to 100% of your marketing strategy will be internet based. As a result, this electronic form of door-knocking is going to save you time and money once you create and put the lead-generating systems into action.

Pay per click budgets can run from $1 to $5000+ per month (for instant gratification of leads). Organic marketing budgets can run from $500 to $2500 per month (long term rewards and hopefully, and in time, the cost decreases).

Compare the **Return on Investment (ROI)** on social/web marketing to traditional advertising, like a newspaper ad. There's so much competition on the page, between the other advertisements and the articles, and it's difficult to monitor who even saw the ad. Whereas, internet marketing such as Pay-per-Click allows you to easily review traffic which is generated by the ad, so you can calculate the ROI and fine-tune the marketing campaign.

Ultimately, when considering ROI and the variations in traffic levels, depending on the website, market, or even the wording of the advert, this reinforces the need for multiple streams of exposure, with multiple nets.

Marketing to Agents on Your Team

A good team leader will make sure all of those nets are cast – it can be expensive, takes a lot of time, constant thinking, figuring out what your competition is doing, what the market is doing, and even if you have an ad, you can't keep the same ad forever...

As a side effect of this smart work, the marketing won't just improve relations with prospective customers, but also has the power to impress potential agents who will want to join the team!

Personal Touch

Regardless of the positives of embracing these 21st Century marketing tools, some agents get so caught up in the tech that they forget the most important rule – you need to give it your personal touch. 98% of buyers and sellers are not going to buy or sell real estate with you without meeting you in person.

All of this is pointless, even if you're reeling in 1000 leads from your IDX website, if you don't open up a door for these people; you won't succeed in your efforts.

Plus, if you only call the prospects 5 days later, and treat them unprofessionally, then you might as well not even bother with the marketing.

Consider this – Over 80% of REALTORS® don't contact a new prospect in the first 24 hours... This is a huge opportunity for YOU.

Something else to consider is that marketing in blogs and sites like Facebook may require more hands-on personal attention so that your audience gets a feel for your true personality. An assistant may have a hard time conveying your characteristics, especially in the beginning. Don't be afraid of spending extra time at the start, in order to put your personal touch on these sites as they will create a valuable first impression of you and your business.

Furthermore, it's possible to go that extra mile to deliver a high touch service – one that will market your business via the best marketing tool available to you: a referral from a satisfied customer.

An example of high touch is sending birthday cards to past and current clients. For instance, instead of an impersonal e-card, we wanted to send something that felt personalized, but still using technology and automation to achieve this. There are companies that will take a sample of your handwriting, turn it into a font, then you can upload a list of your clients' DOBs and their mailing addresses. This company will then schedule the birthdays into a calendar, and when the time comes, they will automatically put this handwritten font into cards and send out a friendly birthday greeting to the client, with a $5 Starbucks voucher.

The result is automated high touch / low time. And if you can master this balance of investing in marketing, without costing yourself too much time, and too much money, then you will be ready for every lead that you generate in the process.

Conclusion

To be successful in both good times and bad, you must invest in your business and a large portion of that is continually and consistently marketing if you want to be in the 100 deals a year league.

Real estate professionals need to touch their market at least 18 times per year to forge a solid memory so people will call you when they are ready to buy or sell. For this reason, it's important to remember the following:

- *Word of mouth and referrals are critical to your business.*
- *Email is an effective, low-cost and trackable way to keep in touch with clients and prospects.*
- *Websites and organic marketing methods are the future of marketing, but never forget the value of personal touch.*
- *With many nets, you can capture the leads, and if speedy and efficient, you can nurture the leads into conversions.*

While you may not be sending out pumpkins anymore, in favor of online organic and pay-per-clicks, the power of marketing continues to be a powerful persuader of prospects and a great capturer of future leads. Ignore it at your own peril, when planning to achieve 100 deals.

Marketing is a valuable and integral ingredient in this book's blueprint.

Read on... Chapter 6: Office Systems – Systemize to Maximize

Chapter 6
Office Systems ~Systemize to Maximize

"Efficiency is doing better what is already being done."
– Peter Drucker, author, management consultant

Naturally, you don't need to use a system if you're only planning to turnover 2 or 3 deals and can wing it to get these deals closed, but when you are considering the volume of 100 deals, a system is imperative and mandatory.

Major businesses constantly look at their production processes to make their companies more efficient and productive. Without the efficiency of office systems, whether you're running a multinational corporation or a local real estate business, it's impossible to maximize your business to its fullest potential.

The first step is making the best use of your time by putting systems in place that will garner showing agent feedback, manage consistent marketing, schedule appointments, communicate with sellers and showing agents, and vastly reduce paperwork.

As a result of these systems and their efficiencies, and by using the right technology, your business should save the cost of at least one to two staff members per year!

Systems You Need to Have in Place
From the top down, there are several basic systems that every office needs to function at any competent level. These include having the latest computer equipment/hardware and software, to having mobile devices for your team – this is the essential infrastructure.

Improvements can be made over time, such as harnessing faster internet speeds and moving to a "cloud computing" model of internet-based computing for sharing resources, software and information. But, in the beginning, for the day-to-day business of getting the doors open and handling sales, the basics will suffice.

When you have the basic structure, you can try and achieve the following:

- *Systemize every process of the office* – *Every process that takes place in your business should be broken down into a numbered step-by-step system.*
- *Create a Business Manual* – *The step-by-step system is turned into a manual for effectively running your office. This way, no step will be forgotten and every team member will be on the same page.*
- *One touch system* – *The goal of creating and organizing this system is to make it "one touch" – and automated.*

The ultimate office is systematically controlled by a one-time touch by one individual, or by one automation feature, and by that one touch it is distributed to the rest of the team, thus creating efficiency. An example of one touch systems have been explained earlier in this book within ShowingSuite.com. We also feel another good example of a one touch system is SendOutCards.com. This website allows a user to set up a client to receive any occasion cards via the web for an infinite period of time. The cards then arrive to the consumer via the mail and can have a font that emulates your personal handwriting. It has many other options as well. I personally used SendOutCards.com extensively in my real estate business. I felt this company exemplified a rare use of high tech and high touch. The cost of service was not inexpensive and I eventually stopped using them so much as it seemed that they stopped growing and listening to the needs of us as users. Contact management was not improving and our world as REALTORS® has been growing more difficult with all the different places we need to input data. As mentioned before, if the technology companies you use don't seem to organically grow with the times, then one is forced to change companies.

As a result, you should have access to:

- *Reports*
- *Office overviews*
- *Individual agent activity*
- *Seller communication*
- *Customer satisfaction data*

- *Website analytics*
- *Lead – Marketing analytics*
- *Feedback status and statistics*
- *Media cost effectiveness*
- *Showings status*
- *Scheduled showings*
- *Listings*
- *Prospects... and more*

This is the power that your business can have, when you harness the whole system not just part of the system.

The Business Manual

The secret to ensuring a fully efficient and well planned step-by-step system is the Business Manual. Each company will have their own unique set of guidelines and steps, tailored to the needs of the geographical real estate market and the skills of the team members. Yet, there are some primary concerns relevant to all REALTORS® which will likely be addressed within the manual's pages...

Ask Yourself:

- *What is your process for hiring?*
- *What is written in your employment contracts?*
- *What are the team member's duties?*
- *How do you handle all of these escrows?*
- *What types of systems do I need to get to 100 deals? E.g. Contact Management software. And how will I evolve them along with my business?*

One of the biggest questions that will spring to mind is, *"How am I going to possibly handle all of these deals?"* This is why you need an action plan in the form of a manual, which is basically a series of checklists of jobs-to-do, in order to smoothly operate and achieve your short and long-term goals.

Step by Step Process

These checklists are 'living' documents – they can be adapted and amended to improve where necessary, to learn by your successes and mistakes. This is why the Business Manual is likely in the form of a virtual digital text, a Google Doc document for instance, which can be evolved along with the lessons and priorities of your business. With Google Documents you can share documents with team members, decide who has editing privileges to help build this manual and share it with your team.

Remember, the key is to keep it simple. Ask yourself if the system will work if a new employee off the street could come in, follow the system, and complete the task. That is the goal.

Here's an example of a simple admin system, placed in a checklist format:

- *Taking a real estate listing*
- *The system begins when the phone call comes in...*
- *The agent calendars the lead...*
- *The lead is then emailed to the agent manager, and the rest of the team.*
- *The system then goes into lead management...*
- *The team/agent is auto-reminded to follow-up on the lead until it "buys or dies."*
- *If the lead/client agrees to a meeting, the appointment is calendared.*
- *Two admin staff members are notified immediately to prepare paperwork and marketing materials...*
- *And so on...*

The reminding in this process is automatically the result of 'ticklers' to keep everything as one-touch as possible. As you can see, if following a checklist system, everything should run like clockwork without ever mishandling a lead or wasting your valuable time.

Office Systems Improve Accountability

Similar to the ABC123 system of categorizing buyer/seller leads as they enter your door, a system is invaluable for tracking and prioritizing what needs to be done in the office, and for tracking what your agents should be doing. If the agent has 10 leads on their plate, they can't be winging it – they need to be following the checklists, and that means you can supervise their progress as they complete the necessary steps.

Transparency will let you know quickly what's not working so you can change with the times. It's amazing how fast something changes when you miss a point on the checklist, which is why these are living, evolving documents that everyone can be aware of. These checklists are there to be tweaked and perfected, and referred to constantly to ensure something hasn't changed to deviate from your expected course.

Take the example of Mark McGwire, the Major League Baseball star (regardless of his controversy) who averaged a homerun once every 10.61 times at bat (the lowest at bats-per-homerun ratio in the history of the game). When he hit a dry spell, he went back and looked at the tapes to see what had changed, what was going wrong. He discovered that he was unknowingly doing something different than he was during the homerun streak. And so Mark went back and tweaked his performance, and started hitting homeruns again...

You've got to tweak the systems to stay on track. This is simple to do, as accountability and transparency are relatively straightforward when there's a system in place. With a system such as ShowingSuite.com, you can actually see which agent has been given the lead, how they're categorized, who is handling how many escrows, etc. The data is right at your fingerprints at any time...

As you're quite likely spending thousands of dollars every month on marketing and staff, it's important to make sure that your pipeline is filled, and that your agents are doing their jobs. The fastest way to tell if your sales team is falling off track, or when your marketing isn't working, is by systemizing the processes into an easy-to-follow and easy-to-follow-up-on checklist.

You don't have millions of dollars to burn as a start-up company, so you must systemize to maximize.

Maximize Your Success – and Maintain It

The systems of communication as you grow your team can become convoluted – who picks up the phone, who makes sure that your agents don't have crossover leads, what do you do if you have a problem?

Every aspect of your business needs a system applied to it. This business is all about one deal at a time and it's also about maintaining the system to keep a constant flow and ensure communication and analysis. Unfortunately in real estate, even when you're doing 100 deals a year for 20 years, the real estate industry will punish you if you take your foot off the pedal for a second. It's possible to go from 100 deals to 10 deals in no time at all, just because a couple of your systems are no longer working efficiently.

Business can be very non-forgiving if you lose your focus. That's the importance of this chapter – it doesn't take much to get completely off track. As you've worked so hard to get to 100 deals, you need to develop and maintain a system to keep you there.

Maintaining is all about oiling the cogs to keep them turning, but it's also related to having a system to maximize this maintenance and make it as one-touch as possible. For instance, every weekend, Alan has an off-site answering service picking up their office phones. Of course, sometimes these services have good people manning the phones, and sometimes it takes a long time for them to answer. If they don't answer well, or it's inconsistent, then they need to know about it. As part of a system, the agent on duty on the weekend is to call and 'test' the service. We ask our on-call agent to try the line about 4 times a day – that's our system to test the system. If they don't answer in 4 rings or less, or they don't say our name correctly, or aren't polite, then our on-call agent asks to speak to their boss immediately to correct it.

You can't let a system break down, so the on-call agent also leaves a message with the service every time, so that we know that they actually called to check... This may seem distrustful, yet it's really about reinforcing the system, and the continuity of your business, as it's far too easy for these little things to fall through the cracks.

Going Paperless
One of the most dramatic, and critical, changes in your Office Systems may be the decision to go "paperless." This will save you dollars, and save the environment in the long-run, but it's a big step and – just like every other system – it needs to have a step-by-step checklist put into place to manage the transition and new process efficiently.

Contact management, interoffice database calendaring and tasks, contracts and deals; these are all affected by a paperless system. Suddenly, all the "paperwork" of the past is moving to a digital format and that means new processes for sharing documents in the office, which may also help to overcome the challenges of getting data while outside of the office. For instance, a digital file can be sent to a Smartphone or mobile device in a way that paper could only be printed and faxed to another fax machine. Now, documents can be stored and manipulated online, making it simpler for collaborating and working as an effective team, such as is available in Google docs or Microsoft's cloud version.

Ultimately, it's now less expensive and less complicated than ever before to go paperless. And the administrational savings speak for themselves... When Alan moved to a paperless Google "cloud" system in 2010, he was previously working with three different servers in the office, spending $1500 to $2000 a month for an individual to maintain the system! Now he spends less than $500 with a more robust sharing and mobile capability...

Of course, paperless only works when the whole team understands it. Sometimes an office will try to go paperless, but the result is doubling their work, because they will print out the files and put them in a filing cabinet as they want something tangible on record... But, this is missing the whole point, and the benefits, of going paperless to maximize time and profits – instead of adding further jobs to your list.

When someone is still demanding paper copies, then this must be addressed with the management. Forcing an agent to maintain digital and paper copies is ludicrous. Remember, the goal is making life easier, not harder!

If you're considering this system for your office, it's never been easier to be completely paperless thanks to today's technologies and tools. This involves scanning and digitizing every aspect of the business. In some cases, it might be worthwhile to build a relationship with a digital firm who will be used throughout your entire company, to make sure everyone is using the same compatible platform and file software.

On a side note, in many states, it's now possible and legal to digitally sign real estate documents. Although it's not like signing with a pen – instead you answer several security questions in order to confirm your identity. This means no more printing, as many customers are getting comfortable with this new practice.

In the end, paperless is more cost effective – you save on toner, paper, new printers and time (as long as you don't print a copy for your records, too!). But, like all of these office systems, you need to first invest the time and energy into establishing them.

Conclusion
If you're going to build a business that handles 100 deals a year, yet you don't want to work 100 hours a week, then there needs to be a solid system in place.

The checklists in the Business Manual can be used as a training tool for new staff in the office; it can help everyone – including you! – stay focused and on the right path to the top... one step at a time.

Read on... Chapter 7: Negotiations

Chapter 7
Negotiations ~ Check, Checkmate

"The universe of negotiation is closer to the world of chess than of war. Both adversaries must follow a certain number of rules."
- Jean-Francois Phelizon, co-author of Chess and the Art
of Negotiation

Our whole business is nothing but negotiation. Negotiating with sellers, other agents, or even your own staff... This is what REALTORS® do all day long.

Yet, negotiation is like a bad word, with negative connotations associated with the act of negotiating and the viewpoint that, in order for one side to gain, the other must lose. But, this needn't be the case in real estate – it doesn't have to be an adversarial battle. In fact, it's possible for everyone to win; the seller, the buyer, and both agents in the equation.

If you are going to make it to 100 deals, you must master the art of negotiating for all of these parties to feel that they succeeded in the negotiation and resulting transaction.

However, before you even get a seat at the negotiating table for a deal, you need to convert the lead into a client. This also requires negotiation on your part, as a potential seller undoubtedly will be looking at your commission versus saving money with discount brokers.

Negotiating Commissions

In order to negotiate, you must present to the client the advantages of working with you to get them to sign you as their listing agent representative.

As there are always going to be discount brokers in the marketplace, you obviously need to be prepared for such questions from the seller. Basically, a seller shouldn't ever be paying you more than discount brokers, unless you can show them your value.

You need to be fully prepared for your Listing Presentation. We will go into further details on this preparation and tips for success in *Chapter 8: Listings ~ There's No Second Place.*

This is your opportunity to show and explain the value that you can offer. The way to do that is prove your track record and negotiation skills, and how they have helped to keep sellers out of trouble and helped bring more monetary value to the table as far as price. In addition, you should highlight how you harness the marketing tools that are available to you, whether it's ads in the paper or on the web. Mention too, your staff who will be assisting in the listing, and you can even talk about the cost of infrastructure of running your business. You must be ready with your value proposition over the competition and present it accordingly.

Naturally, with each item that you discuss, it's important to be prepared to explain how this item affects their end result. There's no point explaining that you have a technological tool, for example, if you don't identify how this tool specifically relates to meeting their goals, adds value, and what it means to them.

Ultimately, without demonstrating the added value, you shouldn't be paid more – and you wouldn't pay more if the tables were reversed. YOU WILL NOT WIN LISTINGS IF YOU CAN'T SHOW TREMENDOUS VALUE.

Demonstrating Value

On a listing presentation, the mention of a discount broker (also known as a "limited service" broker) may never enter the conversation, but count on the fact that 100% of the time it is on the mind of that seller. When being compared to a discount broker, you should always differentiate based on your experience, abilities, knowledge of the geographical market, and technology/tools of your office; any advantage you feel that you have over your listing agent competitors.

Of course, these differentiations will vary on an agent by agent basis, but if you've been a REALTOR® for some time, then we recommend talking about your **Track Record.**

What are your stats? Find out who you are competing against, and compare your records. If it's an agent who has only been in the business for a couple of years, try to find out what that agent's production is, to compare them, experience to experience.

That's the competitive advantage for a long-time, larger real estate business. But, as this book is for REALTORS® from all walks of life, and levels of experience from beginner to pro, you need to find out what your competitive advantage is. The trick is to be creative and think about what distinguishes you over the other guy who runs the full page ads in the paper. For instance, you might mention that you know that neighborhood inside and out, even though you've only sold 2 houses; they were both in this specific area and very similar to theirs.

While one agent can proudly say they've negotiated 300 deals in the last 18 months, a smaller agent may state that they've negotiated deals right on this block, plus, *"I have all the time in the world, this listing will be treated with kid gloves when we have an offer, I'm not part of a big machine..."*

If you know you're running against an agent who is larger than you, you will likely want to talk about the advantages of being small – you're versatile and attentive, you offer a personal touch, and the client won't be lost amongst many other clients. Meanwhile, if you're a large and established REALTOR®, that's what you're fighting against.

Be ready and pick your side before you go into a negotiation. Are you up against a rival, a smaller agent, or a larger agent? Either way, if the clients aren't telling you 'yes' at the end of the presentation, then these factors came up in their minds, but you didn't overcome them.

Highlighting Other Values

In addition to your track record, you may also want to talk about your **Marketing Advantage.** What do you do better than the majority out there? How does the public find out about this listing? Where do you post and advertise? What other services do you offer? Do you utilize Home Feedback or Showing Suite?

Highlight and Differentiate. That's the secret to negotiating and getting the client. For example, discount brokers are notorious for their horrible

communication – they'll sign you up and you won't hear from them again. Highlight how you will be communicating with the client on a regular basis. Show them the transparency that they will have during the listing, as well; they may be impressed to learn about how you will communicate information to them, such as, *"I'm going to provide a seller web portal so you can see all the activity that happens on your house – this is how it's going to be different."*

With the **technology** that you have invested into this process, you can show the potential client that you're different from all the other agents who only utilize MLS. Additionally, talk about each staff member in your office and what they do (or, if you don't have any staff, talk about the office and assets that you have at your disposal).

Invest in understanding the seller's experience in their local market, and what that market is offering. If you don't know, then how would you know how to be different?

By the conclusion of the Listing Presentation, there should be no doubt in the seller's mind why you're special and unlike the competition. Therefore, the next agent that they interview cannot possibly do more than you can do for them. Their question of whether they want to save $5000 on a commission should be answered by this realization that you're the right type of negotiating agent who they want to represent their property when that offer comes in…

On every Listing Presentation, you have to overcome any of their doubts that going with a full-service commission is the best decision they'll ever make. Consequently, if you truly want to be 100% sure that you will succeed in a negotiation of commission versus a discount broker, you should get the tools that you need to win these deals and deliver the results the sellers are looking for.

> Alan says: *"For myself and many agents nationally, even though we don't charge more than the typical agent, it's worth it for a seller to pay much more for what they receive from us. The amount of marketing, experience, knowledge, negotiation power, staff, industry influence and risk avoidance advice is worth a fortune in itself and will net the seller more money, while selling in the least amount of days on market. However, rather than charging more, we simply pride ourselves on providing the best services at the best values in our marketplace. When we represent buyers, we can't begin to tell you how many $$ we have saved for our clients… and even more importantly, how many mistakes we have stopped buyers*

from making. Buyers need to be extremely concerned about the right neighborhood, right lot, etc.

In addition, we are always trying to compare and improve the professionalism of our industry to match the very best of professionals in other industries. Now while I truly don't enjoy mentioning attorneys, I feel that there are many common threads between the ways our industries relate to our clients; also within the infrastructure of our businesses, staff, marketing, etc. With that said, wouldn't it be great if our industry demanded a retainer for our time before use... similar to an attorney?

My dear friend had one legal experience which required him to hire an attorney. He hired someone that seemed competent, and was almost half the hourly cost of the more reputable attorneys in town. What happened thereafter was a nightmare. Not only was he losing what should have been a slam dunk case, but he was being charged a fortune, because the low priced attorney was working so many extra and unnecessary hours, while making mistakes at the same time. The mess continued and got out of hand, so my friend fired this individual and hired one of San Diego's leading attorneys, at literally double the hourly fee. Paul's experience and knowledge was unmatched. Within a short period of time, the case was handled successfully and finished.

That old saying, 'you get what you pay for' is always true as we compare service industries. I find that our industry is no different. As I watch sellers and buyers make mistakes because they attempt to save a few dollars on a several hundred thousand or even multi-million dollar transaction, it just doesn't make sense to me. It would be wonderful if there were some universal handbook available to all sellers and buyers teaching them what questions to ask in order to choose the very best agent for the job of selling or buying their next home."

Perception of Value

Following the Listing Presentation, if the decision isn't going in your favor and the potential client says 'No', you must not be afraid to ask them why they don't want to list with you. For instance, is it because of the commission?

However, what we've learned a long time ago is that there was a time when many REALTORS® would fight for a commission they didn't deserve, because they didn't have the value that was needed. It can be a tough sale when you're trying to earn 6%, but you don't have anything to offer. Remember – **value is a perception**. The client needs to perceive that value as an extraordinary one.

This is why we've decided in our real estate companies to create so much value in our Listing Presentations that nobody would consider 6% an overpriced rip-off. That's the key to negotiating and winning the listing, and getting one step closer to closing another one of your 100 deals.

Listing Paperwork

Of course, until the ink is dry on the paperwork, no listing is secure. As a seller might interview as many as five agents (or more) before settling on the actual agent to sell their house, it's important to get the paperwork filled out, preferably after the Listing Presentation and in person to officially close the listing deal.

If they won't commit, try this technique to close. We call it the 99 Question Close. It goes like this:

> *"Mr. & Mrs. Seller, I understand you want to think over listing with myself and my firm, but while I am here I can get some information, so all I need is a call and we can hit the ground running faster on selling your home. Does that sound fair? Great!"*

Then you go through every listing question that is imaginable, from the number of bedrooms, down to the number of gallons per flush of their toilets, the type of water heater, etc. Fill out all the disclosures and the listing agreement, and post date it for two days in the future.

Typically, we would ask them to fill out the paperwork, *"While we're all here, and then call me if you want to go ahead with it."* Or, *"Fill it out, and if you're not 100 % comfortable in the next few days, just call me to cancel it."* Naturally, once they've filled out this lengthy paperwork and answered all your questions, most people don't want to go through this listing paperwork torture again!

By the time they're done signing, they're happy that it's over.

Negotiating a Deal

George Costanza once walked into a little fruit market as he tried to explain to his friend Jerry Seinfeld that everything in life is negotiable. To prove his point, George approached the owner of the store and started trying to bargain over the price of a piece of fruit. Yet, the owner wasn't impressed, became irate and soon demanded that George, *"Get out of my store!! Get out and never come back!"*

Shaking his head, George considers the deal. *"Never come back? Well, how about a week, can I come back in a week?"* *"No!"* shouts the irate owner of the fruit store.

"How about in two weeks?" *"No!"*

"How about a month?" George pleads. *"Okay, one month, but no sooner"* the owner agrees with a nod.

"See, Jerry," George says with a knowing smile. *"Everything's negotiable."*

George is right and it's your job as a REALTOR® to have this mindset as you enter into negotiations with buyers and agent-to-agent. For the most part, it's crucial to know: what is the buyer and seller's motivation? This will drive the entire deal.

Of course, when it's a commercial deal, it's all about the numbers. But, when it's residential, it's a home and that's emotional.

Also, we have to remember what our role is. As real estate agents, we're not the owners of the property. The sellers have the ultimate decision to make, and it's our job to give good information and guide them. But, we can't take responsibility with what happens in the market, and we needn't pretend that we know what will happen with it either. Certainly, you can't stop the seller's neighbors from putting their home up for sale, at a 5% lower price!

Yet, for a buyer, this might be just the news they need to negotiate a better price for their dream home...

Representing Buyers

Our industry has changed in recent years as we now sign buyer brokerage agreements, in the same way sellers sign listing agreements. This has dramatically evolved the way we negotiate with the seller and negotiate with the buyer.

Previously, without such an agreement, agents were scared to talk honestly and strongly with their client. To be frank, it was difficult to be blunt as we feared they wouldn't want to work with us again, or might even back out of the deal and hire someone else to negotiate. However, after signing a buyer brokerage agreement, the agent has protection against such behavior, so agents are able to negotiate and convey their thoughts to their buyers more freely.

This is important when a client's expectation of getting a home for their offered price is unrealistic. Whereas, in the old days, an agent used to deliver a convoluted message when a client balked at paying a certain price for a home.

Thus, buyer brokerage agreements are critical, and we won't enter negotiations without one. Yet, to sign a buyer, once again you must negotiate and share the value of signing that agreement – let them know, *"We're going to spend the time now working for you, so we need to be exclusively representing you."* Have a brief buyer presentation to show them, similar to your listing presentation, and at the close, ask for the signature on the buyer brokerage agreement.

On a side note, it should be theoretically much easier to sign a buyer, as 99.9% of the time in residential purchases it will be the sellers, not them, writing the commission check for your work. Nevertheless, if it's possible to get in front of a buyer – not on the phone or via email – they should be more inclined to sign that contract. You want them to feel a bond with you, and it helps to explain face-to-face these advantages of hiring you, instead of them bouncing around from agent to agent like in a pinball machine.

Just like a good lawyer, many buyers want a good real estate agent to represent them. Although, with 20 different REALTORS® in the paper alone, they often don't see anything wrong with going from one agent to the next. You must show your strengths of representing them in the presentation kit (explored further in *Chapter 9: Buyer Presentations*).

By the way, if they don't sign this agreement, then you've just saved yourself a world of time, as they planned on using and abusing you, and driving you nuts! They may have a sister, brother, or relative in-law, in another county, who is planning to negotiate the deal and you're just being used to show the homes. They want a free ride and then they'll get their cousin to write up the deal!

Once this paperwork is signed, then we can negotiate hard with that seller. As always, we will take into account whether it's a fast, slow or flat market. This makes all the difference.

Sometimes when the market is hot, you just want your offer accepted – there might be five other offers on the table, and while you want a good price, it's likely most important that the buyer get that property, as they lost the last three properties they wanted…

As a result, you should have your finger on the pulse of the market and have a solid awareness of the value of property in your region, in order to help improve your negotiating for sellers and buyers.

Decline the First Offer
Should you say no to the first offer? That's a difficult question and will depend on the specifics of a situation. Though, there are good reasons for negotiating to make everyone feel like they got a deal – as opposed to grabbing the first offer and making the buyer feel like they overpaid, or the seller feeling forced to take a quick deal like they were robbed!

When appropriate, it can be healthy to negotiate a little bit – even if you're not far off an ideal price and terms. You can ask about closing a week earlier, or that they use your escrow company, or even request another $500 off the price… But, remember, this isn't about jeopardizing the deal, it's about solidifying it!

The ultimate goal is to make the buyer feel good about their purchase, and the seller, too! Everybody needs to feel a win-win on the deal.

That being said, it used to be a concern that buyers would feel like they overpaid, due to the price-tag on properties being higher. In a slower economic climate, we need to make sure sellers don't feel like they undersold. You need to be on their side, in a "consultative/option" mindset; make sure they're aware of all of their options, narrow it down to the best one and explain why, then ask what they want to do.

Moreover, it's pertinent to reinforce to sellers the risks of holding on to a home today. They can wait for a better price, but it's always a risk that the offers won't get any better, and could get worse. But, that also doesn't mean that you should snatch up a terrible offer without sleeping on it. You can share this sentiment with the buyers by letting them know when they send in a low-ball offer: *"That's a lot lower than what they want… We need an extra day to consider this offer… this is a shock."* Usually, they will give you an extra day before returning to the negotiation to adjust or close the deal.

While it may sometimes seem like buyers and sellers are on different sides of the board, like in chess, in fact all of the strategy is working towards the same result – a closed deal, exchanging money for a property. We're all on the same side. But, like George says, on the road to getting this result, *"everything is negotiable."*

Agent to Agent Negotiation

There's an interesting quandary in the real estate industry, as many envision the agent-to-agent negotiations as hostile and adversarial. But, you can attract more flies with a teaspoon of honey than you can with a jar of vinegar. Besides, there is actually a sentiment of let's play by the rules and have a good match. This means we always want to leave on a good note even if negotiations fall through, as who knows if they will be back next week with a new offer!

First and foremost, always negotiate for your client, and not for your own profit. And always put ego in the back pocket, otherwise you could eliminate the possibility of this deal working out. Finally, remember to do everything you can to make everybody feel good about what's happening. If you are doing 100 deals a year the chances are you are going to work with this client and this agent again.

There doesn't need to be a loser in a negotiation, if both sides are striving for a win-win situation.

Read on… Chapter 8: Listings ~ There's No Second Place

Chapter 8
Listings ~ There's No Second Place

"Second place sucks."
- Alan Shafran and Rick Bengson

In the world of listings, the silver medal means absolutely nothing. It pays less than nothing. And, in fact, it actually costs you, because of all those wasted hours (and gas for your car, materials for the listing presentation, etc).

This is why your only goal in the business of getting a real estate listing is first place. Being second carries zero reward – and even a negative balance. Whereas, if there were five REALTORS® competing for the same listing, then the last person actually beat you, because they probably spent less of their time and money on it!

Although, of course, for any agent aiming for the magic number of 100 deals, this drive to first place applies in every area of your business. Essentially, you've got to be great at prospecting to get the lead, nurturing the lead, then closing the lead for an appointment, *and* then closing the appointment against your competition for a listing or a buyer, *and* then getting them to sell/buy their home, *and* getting them to escrow to close, too. Meanwhile, if you're lacking in any of these areas, or missing a single piece of that puzzle, then the whole machine will break down…

Be Number 1
The mindset of the REALTOR® must always be fixated on the concept, *"I've got to get this or this is a huge waste of my time."* For both of us, this attitude of being first, and second place being unacceptable, has been instrumental in getting to the top and maintaining our position. It takes dedication and concentration, as

well as awareness. For years, we listened to our clients when they told us how often a competitor followed up on a lead – this is the kind of intel that we needed to ensure we were out-performing, out-servicing and receiving outstanding results above our competition.

Naturally, it's one thing to find yourself placed second in your market; for example, if you sold 100 homes and someone else sold 125. Yet, when you're in the running for a listing, you need to be first in the eyes of the customer. The only way to guarantee this is by leading with a listing presentation that is worthy of that pole position.

Unless the client is referred (otherwise known as a "come list me"), a presentation can be critical to sealing the deal (and then you still have to sell the home!). The key to every presentation is answering one question: *"What's the advantage that sets you head and shoulders above your competitors and how does that formulate to value or more $$$ for the seller?"*

You need to pick a path, make a plan, and have it ready for the clients to consider. Whether you're a one person operation or part of a 20 person team, you need to differentiate yourself and highlight the benefits of going with you versus the other guy or gal.

In a presentation, like a lawyer in a courtroom who is building a case for their client, you are building a case for yourself to ask for the order and represent them in probably the largest transaction of their life to date. As we've mentioned, each agent is different – what assets you have to offer will vary from person to person, office to office. Here's a list of points to consider mentioning in your presentation, if applicable to the case for why they should hire you or your company... today.

- *Size and efficiency of a large team vs. intimacy of a small operation*
- *Years in the business*
- *Years living in the area*
- *Number of sales that your team does in a year (100, eventually!)*
- *Less sales = more time to spend on this listing*
- *More sales = more experience*
- *Marketing techniques*
- *Service*
- *Availability*
- *Local statistics*

The Price is Right?

Pricing is the single most critical point of the listing… it doesn't matter what you do for marketing, if the price isn't right, good luck!

So, why not highlight your pricing strategy during your presentation? But don't forget that, while a client will want to get top dollar for their house, overpricing can be detrimental to your career, as well as significantly reduce the homeowner's prospects of a reasonably quick sale.

The Overpriced Pig

There's an old saying in the Stock Market: *"What gets fat? Bears, bulls and pigs – bulls make money, bears make money, and pigs get slaughtered…"*

When the home listing is not priced correctly and realistically, based on comparable homes in the neighborhood and the market in general, then you will be spending your time and the expense of your staff's time by taking an overpriced listing. Moreover, the consumers who see your listing – potential clients who are considering your company for their business – will see that you aren't able to sell that listing and their estimation of you will lower dramatically.

Let's say in 120 days, if that listing doesn't sell, then you might have spent $5000 on marketing. Logically, you're not buying full page glossy magazine ads for a two bedroom, one bath house, yet it still adds up – not to mention, the cost to your reputation and the ongoing relationship with the current client who will soon be anxious about selling their home.

Although this might seem like an easy task, it actually is quite a challenge to show and convince a seller that the market value of their home is $50,000 less than what they expected, have them agree with you, and sign the listing agreement at the same time. Your presentation skills need to be crystal clear, simple, straight forward, and sincere. The presentation itself needs to make complete logical sense to the extent where the seller can't argue with you. Good questions to ask sound like this: *"Mr. and Mrs. Seller, today, you are the seller of this home. But, after it sells, you will become a buyer. Let's take the buyer's stance on the current marketplace and your home's value. I know both of you are quite savvy – what would you pay for this home if you were an actual buyer and why?"*

Last but not least, nothing will matter more than the seller's motivation to sell their home. If they have no motivation, you can be perfect in your presentation, prove all the right points, ask all the right questions, and nothing will matter; they will probably still overprice their home considerably.

Keep things in perspective when judging your results. I have found that it is best to leave an overpriced or unmotivated seller with a great impression and wish them the best of luck with a different REALTOR®. I look to keep communication open so that if they want to hire me in the future, after the first listing agent fails, they will feel comfortable enough to contact me for another appointment. We talk about this more below.

Pricing for Buyers

When a house is freshly listed, there's an opportunity to attract the host of buyers who are actively searching in your marketplace. If your house fits within their parameters, and they believe it is priced at a good value, then the system works; if it's overpriced, many people won't bother even looking inside the front door...

If that's the case – and we're dealing with an overpriced home that doesn't match the parameters of the current home-seekers – that means we're looking for a new buyer who wants to move. But, we have to wait for them because we've exhausted the big market. This is far from ideal; therefore, if we don't price the listing right for the big market today, we could be waiting for quite a while – and this is the number one reason for an expired listing.

Moreover, you may think we can price it high and if someone low-balls after a while, then they will reduce the price and I can sell this listing. To give further insight into the mentality of today's buyer, they tend to avoid low-balling. They think it's insulting to the seller (and it can be, sometimes). Instead of making low offers on a high-priced property, they would rather not make the offer at all – or even set foot inside the building if they can't afford it and risk emotionally attaching themselves to a home beyond their budget.

An example would be listing a home for $899,000 and not receiving any offers. However, if you lower the price to $875, you may get three. Why were these three buyers not willing to make an offer at $899? This is the mindset of buyers today and this needs to be explained to sellers during your listing presentation's pricing component. Buyers out there have come to understand that they're wasting their time and the REALTOR®'s time getting emotionally connected and committed to a home they're not going to get.

Say, if the buyer's home budget is $600,000 and they're looking at a home priced at $700, then they know that most likely that seller is looking to get at least $675 or higher. This is out of their price range and often the buyer gets sick of being locked out of a deal after 2 or 3 times of trying. Therefore, the buyers will only look at homes now that are priced around $625. Bear this in mind if your sellers are considering a listing price of $650,000, for instance, yet they're willing to sell at $600, because they will be missing the best buyers who won't consider homes in the $650s range.

Furthermore, when you price at $650, in this example, then you're probably competing against homes that are actually worth more than yours, who are looking to sell at $650.

Naturally, it can be difficult to explain this to the greedy and unrealistic seller who is uneducated about the market, but it's part of your job and it will make everyone's life easier to have all these cards on the table from the beginning. You will be respected for it and it will actually help you get that listing.

At the end of the day, the real problem with overpriced listings is not the seller, it's the agent – if they're willing to take it and willing to be sold by the sellers as to why to take it, all they're doing is ruining their business. Don't be one of those agents. You're missing out on that initial market. And you don't want to see this home, and your reputation, languishing for months in the public's eye. It's bad for the home, bad for the sellers, and bad for business.

Remember – if you have an ethical responsibility to that seller, it's to make sure they understand that by pricing that high it could actually cost them 5% or more of what the end result sales price could be. If they don't understand it, you need to explain it.

Bottom-line – you always want to be a good advocate for them. Sometimes that will mean standing your ground and not just going with the high price. Show them the comparables and explain your pricing suggestions. Explain your reasoning via an educational format and you will take more listings – additionally, these will be listings that will sell and put you on pace to that 100 deals.

Different Ways to Price
There are several options for pricing in California and New York, which are beginning to catch on across the nation. The usual practice is the standard traditional pricing, where there is a single price, e.g. asking $700,000. Although, there is a new practice which originated in Australia, and spread to California, known as VRM – variable range marketing.

VRM is when you list a home in a pricing range, e.g. seller will entertain offers from $649 to $700. The purpose of that range is when a buyer or agent looks on the Multiple Listing Service website, if they search anywhere between $640-750, this home will show up regardless. Thus, opening up more properties for that search and a larger potential market for that VRM-priced property.

Of course, the success of VRM depends on the climate of the marketplace you're in – if you're in a depressed marketplace, then you need to be careful that buyers' agents are not only focusing on the lower end of the price scale; if the market is up, you will be hoping to push above the high end, or get multiple offers.

The last type of pricing is bidding, an auctioneer type of pricing, e.g. home is worth $700 but you list it at $599 with a concept that you're under pricing and we will look at the very best offers in the next week. Perhaps you would even list at $499 to get a massive amount of attention, like 30 or 40 offers, then ask for a best and final counter offer from everyone. This can be successful, depending on the market. It worked in Silicon Valley in the dotcom days, but it can be fairly risky and expensive for the seller if the end results are not positive.

Nevertheless, most of North America is predominantly using the traditional type of pricing format, because the access to the other options is dictated by MLS as their computer systems need to accommodate the variable range market, for example. Even REALTOR.com recently implemented variable range into their structure, so it is making an impact slowly but surely. Meanwhile, most of the regional MLS systems will only allow one price to be put in there, but it pays to be aware of developments that may potentially become available in your area in the future, so you can be the first riding high atop the tide of change.

Multiple Offers
Generating multiple offers is possible, whether you're in a fast or slow market...

HomeFeedback.com can show you how – in a fast market, we can let every agent who has shown this property know that we have an offer coming in, with a deadline to make a decision by Friday. We would automatically send an email to every agent who showed this home to their clients and advise them, *"Now would be a great time to make an offer."*

For example, our email would say something along the lines of: *"Jim, you had shown the property at 123 Thunder Road. We are expecting an offer, so we're entertaining other offers until 3:00pm tomorrow. Please let me know if your client will be making an offer."* This email also has photos of the property so they can easily remember it, as well as all of our contact information.

Or, in another example, God forbid we put a home into escrow and the buyers back out of the deal for a reason beyond our capabilities. With my HomeFeedback system, everyone who saw your house can be emailed in 5 minutes to say we're back on the market, and again it's a great time to write offers as the home is now available to your buyers. This is also a good feature to show on a listing presentation to highlight that you have a plan in case of an emergency.

While in a slow market, you can drop the price by $5000 and similarly email everyone to let them know in an instant, to hopefully generate a multiple offer situation. The email is like this: *"Jim, you had shown the property at 123 Thunder Road to your buyers – we just dropped the price by $5,000 and expect a lot of activity. This would be a great time for your clients to make an offer."*

Not to mention the other benefits of this system – it's truly amazing how well it works for keeping the seller informed about all activity related to their home listing. We can give them the feedback and the transparency, via their own personal log-in, so they can see for themselves every showing that takes place, see every contact that is made with the agents involved, see the comments directly from them, as well as the statistics on the property feedback; basically, enabling all of us to analyze what we need to do to sell that house. Sellers will even ask <u>you</u> for a price reduction after viewing their feedback, comments and statistics.

You can tell them in your presentation, *"You'll have an insight on what's happening with your house 24/7."* For instance, the seller can even have control over the showings by blocking out times on an online calendar. If they have a birthday party coming up on Saturday afternoon, they can guarantee that no showings get scheduled during that time.

Of course, it would be wise to highlight these types of technological tools that will be provided to the sellers by showcasing them in your listing presentation. You must explain to them what you can do, because if you have those tools and you don't share that, what good are they? You pay for the service, you should be making bank with it.

It's an education, as almost none of these sellers will know about this stuff. This is why we recommend that you always have some tech tools in your listing presentation, aside from what MLS has for everybody. *"This is how I'm different and better."*

These tools, and your overall presentation, can set you apart from the rest, so you can be the best – and get the home listed right there and then.

Staging

When taking on a new listing, you will invariably need to look around the home and this is a perfect time to prepare a staging report of what a seller needs to do to sell. Most sellers have lived in their abode for too long, and they're too close to it. Whereas you can provide a subjective opinion and let them know about any pitfalls that can be fixed before they jeopardize an offer.

For example, some homes need to be warmed up because they're so sterile, others need to clean the dog poop off the floor. Either way, it's imperative to have a report of your recommendations in order to protect yourself later and/or confirm your professionalism. Ultimately, as you begin the selling process, you will receive comments on the house and if someone says that it is unclean or there are old appliances, you can remind the seller that we talked about this, *"I did my job. You chose not to fix it and that's fine, but I did my job."*

In the case of staging, you may also need to suggest furnishing the home if the seller will not be living there anymore. By placing furniture in the rooms, potential buyers will be able to envision themselves moved in and living there.

This used to be a costly option for sellers, but things have changed. Staging companies are becoming very creative, more flexible and more affordable than they used to be. Still, as it was in the old days, there are traditional stagers who charge based on each piece of furniture, with a minimum of a 90 day commitment. As a result, a small amount of furniture can cost a seller $2,500-$3,000 a month. While today, the new breed of stagers can facilitate a fully staged home, top to bottom, for a period of 5-6 months, for a cost to the seller of roughly ½ a percent of the list price, payable upon closing only.

The new way of doing things requires the home to be vacant, of course, and the staging company hires a 'home manager' who lives there for free, no rent, but this person purchases the furniture from the stagers. Essentially, the stagers have figured out a way to make their money through other avenues. This means that the home is staged and — another benefit for those with a vacant home on the market — there will be someone caring for it, making sure it's in good condition and available for showings.

Why List Today?

○━⊸ This is a big question at the end of every listing presentation. Time is of the essence, but the decision to list will depend on one factor alone – **the Seller's Motivation is always more important than the Agent's Motivation.**

Seller's Motivation will always win. If the Agent's Motivation to sell is higher than the Seller's, the Seller will eventually change their mind when things get rough.

This is one of the biggest mistakes that agents make. If they try and get someone to move who isn't 100% convinced to do so, their job is impossible. A home is too much of a big ticket item.

Buying and selling a house is an enormously daunting task to most clients. They won't follow through, unless they need to. Which means the seller won't listen to your advice, unless they need to sell. Their motivation needs to be substantial, so you need to always see things from their perspective: *Why should they list today? What's their motivation?*

Only when their motivation is substantial can you can talk about short term and long term decisions, which applies to every facet of the financial marketplace. Short term decisions are risky, so you have to think long term. Today, they can get a certain price for their home, but if they are certain about selling in the next 6 months to a year, then they should list their home today, rather than roll the dice when their home could be worth considerably less down the road.

Market conditions are never set in stone and the slightest change in their neighborhood can affect the price, too. For example, a neighbor could be desperate to sell and puts their home on the market at a price much lower than your seller was ever considering. Who knows what will happen tomorrow? Yes, a home could be worth more in a year's time, but it could also be worth much less – that's a risk that a seller takes when he decides to play the waiting game.

The message that we convey to sellers is that there is always the possibility that you could lose money on your home when you wait. Your home is not a liquid asset; you can't press a button and make your money back.

Thus, we counsel sellers that it's often a better choice to sell now, rather than be pressured by the situation of needing to sell in the future. Truly, it can cost dearly when they <u>need</u> to sell, rather than selling at a time that gives them room to breathe. For starters, they don't get to sell at market rate if they need to sell quickly and urgently – they need to sell below market to get it done fast. This should be a consideration for them when deciding to list sooner, rather than later.

Why List with YOU Today?

Many sellers will want to reflect on your listing presentation and possibly interview other candidates for the job. But why, when they've already found the best REALTOR®? This is what you need to reiterate in order to close the listing and get on with the real work of selling their home.

- *We've been sitting here for four hours; do you want to do it again with someone else?*
- *I'm here right now. Here's the paperwork. Call me tomorrow if you change your mind.*
- *What do you think another REALTOR® is going to do more than me?*
- *If you were 100% sure I was the best, would you proceed?*
- *Do you want to go over this again with two more agents? Also, the more agents you interview, the more enemies you're creating as you have to reject and might offend them. As a result, what if they won't bring their clients to see your home?*
- *Make one decision and move on, then you don't have to deal with any of that.*

In a best case scenario, you want to be the first agent through the door. Some REALTORS® strive to be the last one, in order to stand out from their competition that was sitting in the same chair before them, to benefit from the seller's learning curve. However, if you're not the first, you might not ever get the chance to be last...

Unless you think you're the biggest dog in the county and people will wait to hear what you have to say, you need to get in there first, before another closer gets in and lists the home.

Closing the Listing – Tips

Consider the following, which might help you to get that listing.

Partner with better known agents – There are many advantages to being on a team, especially when you can go into a listing presentation and sell your partnership, or even name your team leader as the co-lister. Let them know that your team has had many sales, does a lot of advertising in the area, etc, and then you can benefit from these assets.

If there's a listing that you think you need help with, it can be very smart to find another REALTOR® who has done well or has more experience in that area (hopefully this is someone within your company). When you share the listing, you also share the commission. This is typical when it's a higher priced listing that you don't have a background in, or you're going into an area that you're not comfortable with. A very well known agent can be like a local celebrity and you can use that celebrity to your benefit. You piggy-back off that agent's name, even though you got the lead and you both share in the commission.

Remember – Sometimes you'll be the well known agent and sometimes you'll be the new agent working your way up. Next time, you can say, *"I sold the $1.5 million house down the street..."* This is a great way to build up your business.

> Alan says: *"The first time I sold an $8 million home, I networked with a team of agents in La Jolla who are dominant in that multimillion dollar home market; this helped me to get the listing. It worked and we all had a fantastic experience. Next thing I knew, I had a substantial market share of multimillion $$ homes up and down the coast. Today, I still have sold the highest priced homes in Carlsbad and Encinitas right on the coastline."*

Partnering can help you solidify your reputation and present yourself in the right way, to look the best. So don't be afraid of bringing in another agent to bolster your credentials and get the listing.

What happens when the seller says:

- **"Your commission is high?"** – *The REALTOR® commission is high because it is factored into the risk involved with expending time, energy, and money on marketing efforts...*
- **"I have other agents to talk to..."** – *I will let them know on your behalf that the home is listed, so you don't have to have that awkward conversation...*
- **"I need to check with my wife... boyfriend... mother... uncle"** – *It's awful when you realize that it's a one-legged presentation and they make excuses about needing to check with someone else. It's happened to all of us – yet, you can still get them to sign and cancel later.*

Certainly, the realization that they don't want to make a decision tonight can be disappointing, yet it doesn't mean that you need to accept 'no' for an answer – at least, not without a "fight"!

This simply means that you need to step it up and close the presentation. Always go for the close. And remember to remind the seller, *"If you think that I'm being aggressive by asking for your order, then isn't that the type of agent you want working for you?"*

Nine out of ten times, that's exactly the type of agent they want representing them, as opposed to the laid-back type who says, *"Okay, I will get back to you tomorrow..."* Instead, you should tell them that you will prove your worth. Find out what it will take to make them certain that you are the only agent for them.

Now You're Listed

The race to get the listing is just the beginning of a potentially long road to seeing that 'For Sale' sign in the yard with your name on it, and eventually the elusive 'Sold' sign. Nevertheless, for you, the listing presentation is 100% about crossing that finish line, which also represents the start of the selling process.

> Alan says: *"Don't ever forget about first place. Before every listing presentation, I would write a big zero on a piece of paper, then draw an anti-sign across it. This reminded me that if I didn't take that listing now, I had zero percent chance of the homeowners calling me back later — It's all or nothing."*

Read on... Chapter 9: Buyer Presentations

Chapter 9
Buyer Presentations

Many agents have and continue to work with buyers without the security of a formal contract. Yet, similar to the Listing Agreement with the sellers, there are Buyer Broker agreements between an agent and the buyer for a specific period of time, with an exclusivity attached to it – that exclusivity basically states that if they buy any home within that period of time, as long as they're in that relationship with us, we will get paid a pre-agreed upon sum of money. In many real estate businesses, it's 3%.

Nevertheless, a big weakness in the real estate business is the fact that we're mostly used and abused as it relates to buyers. Some buyers are confused as to how we get paid – they think that as long as the agent opens up the door, someone's paying the agent, and they don't really care who. Nothing could be further from the truth, but that doesn't stop agents from spinning the roulette wheel and wasting their valuable time with buyers who aren't loyal to them.

It's not totally the fault of the buyers, who often don't know any better. Instead, as agents, we could do a much better job of explaining to the buyers both our expectations and our terms under which we'll work, not to mention how their behavior does and does not affect us.

The first problem is the majority of agents <u>assume</u> that buyers know how the process works. As usual, this assumption makes an 'ass' out of 'u' and 'me.' By assuming these people looking for a house know how everyone gets paid, you're on a one-way ticket to getting used without receiving a single red cent. And even if the buyer has bought a home before, and it may have been 10 years ago, the buyer doesn't likely remember how everything plays out.

We whole-heartedly recommend explaining the in's and out's before going in there and asking for a buyer brokerage. The perfect situation is to arrange a Buyer's meeting, akin to the Listing Presentation.

Alan is one of the few people who teaches REALTORS® about buyer brokerages across the country. It's a topic that agents are very afraid to broach in a conversation with the buyer. Too often the thinking is, *"If I can just get the buyers in the home and they'll love it, then I can get a quick sale"* – but what are the buyer's rights?

In many jurisdictions, they could call up any agent and ask to be shown as many homes as they want, and then decide to call the listing agent on the property they just viewed and ask that agent to write up the offer! In fact, they even have the right as a buyer today to have one agent write up the contract, decide that agent isn't doing a good job for them, fire them in the middle of negotiations, and hire the listing agent or another agent who's willing to cut their commission – believe us when we tell you, this happens every day. The one thing that stops these kinds of shenanigans is the buyer brokerage agreement.

Procuring Cause – R.I.P.
There is a REALTOR® ethics rule called Procuring Cause, which would protect us as agents amongst our industry just for being the first agent to show and/ or identify a home to a buyer. Essentially, you could win the argument that you deserved the commission, if you could prove you introduced a buyer to a listing in any form or fashion, and those buyers decided to buy – not through you, the introducing agent, but another agent entirely. As a result, you could sue for half the commission! But this is no longer as clear cut as it used to be. Buyers are still the consumers and without the proper agency agreements signed, the agent loses a tremendous amount of protection if the buyer chooses to change agents almost any time before a transaction is consummated. Of course, each troublesome scenario has its own details which differ from others... Nonetheless, we are left with an even greater need for some kind of exclusive agreement between buyers and their agents.

Why a Contract?

When we started out in this business, the Buyer Broker contract wasn't even available from the California Board of REALTORS® – though, they now have a clear-cut template. Back in the day, we created our own contract, loosely written, yet ensuring that both buyer and agent were on the same page with each other's expectations.

The Benefits of a Buyer Brokerage to the Agent

- *Your propensity for getting taken advantage of is a lot higher when you don't have one.*
- *You're having an upfront conversation with the buyer.*
- *You're better off going to a movie than helping a buyer without an agreement.*
- *Without one, you have to be available 24/7 because you're scared they will jump ship at any time.*
- *If you have a brokerage agreement, you can sleep a little easier.*

An example of a buyer broker agreement saving the day? There are many horror stories of what can happen without one.

> <u>Alan says</u>: *"One time a home was in escrow, after the buyer (who had signed with me) was somehow manipulated into using another agent to make an offer. I simply called the other agent and told him to send over the escrow documents. He was shocked at first until I explained that the buyer was already in a buyer broker contract with me! It's rare, but for the times when it happens, you are a believer in the buyer broker agreement forever."*

Of course, there are a multitude of benefits for the buyer, too. And these need to be made apparent during the Buyer Presentation.

The Buyer Presentation – Tips and Points for Inclusion

Nowadays we focus our Buyer Presentations on the benefits we can offer them, in particular, the technology and tools at our disposal. However, the old way to present to buyers is deeply-rooted in the industry – known as the ABC's of Real Estate Service, i.e. what most REALTORS® do:

*A*dvertise *homes in order to get buyers to call them.*

*B*eg *buyers to come in and talk with them.*

Choose a bunch of homes you think they will like.

Drive them from house to house showing them dozens of homes.

Encourage the buyer to make an offer on every house you see.

Feel frustrated because the homes are not to their liking.

Get on your knees and pray that they will buy something after all that hard work.

Instead, we recommend focusing on the Buyer's unique needs:

Step 1:
Find out how much they can afford (by helping the Buyer get Home Loan Pre-Approval).
Step 2:
Send the Buyer information on homes that match their criteria (our unique Buyer Profile Service).
Step 3:
Help them get the home they want using your Specialized Knowledge.

This helps buyers to get the best financing, so they know exactly how much they can afford, eliminating wasted time looking at homes that are under or over their price range; this also means they can make a stronger offer when they find the right property.

The Benefits for a Buyer
- *The Buyer will be working with somebody who is truly required to represent their main interests and needs.*
- *Ethically, they are hiring an exclusive buyer broker, and this person must do a certain job for them.*
- *There's more to buying homes than opening the door — without a skilled buyer's agent with experience and knowledge of the market, the buyer is missing out on their negotiating skills during the buying and closing process. Remember —when you have an agent who has been negotiating for 25*

years, they can save you a lot more. And this negotiation is never over till the keys are in the hands of the buyer.

A buyer also needs to understand how loyalty is a two-way street. They might think it's smarter to play the field and not sign with any agents. Yet, the buyer who is looking at homes with 5 separate agents is actually working with nobody – none of these agents is loyal to them. Who will bother to share a great new listing with this buyer, when they have other buyers who have signed exclusive agreements?

Yes, any buyer could decide to take the shotgun approach of working with multiple agents, while handling the home search on their own – visiting all the different websites, scheduling a load of viewings by themselves. But why would you do that, when you could have someone who you trust, coordinating it all, finding out what your needs are, with access to all of the inventory and helping you narrow the options down to the perfect home?

Ultimately, the Buyer Presentation needs to state explicitly, *"I'm going to find the best home for your needs, I'm going to negotiate the lowest price, I'm going to secure the best financing, and finally meet your home-buying needs with the least amount of hassle."*

It's a total hassle when you're doing it all yourself – why would any buyer want to act like an agent, when they don't save anything? This is why a buyer brokerage can make sense, when explained properly to a buyer. You get a professional working on your behalf, dedicated to your needs and goals – and it won't cost you a penny.

The buyers pay us absolutely no fees for our services. The seller will pay our <u>entire</u> commission on the home that is purchased. *"All we ask for in return is your loyalty."*

Make Them Your Priority

It's all about priorities. Typically, it's ideal when a buyer calls us and says, *"I want to work with you exclusively, but make me your priority and give me first shot at every new listing that meets my needs."* This is far better than the one who says, *"I'm working with 6 agents – first one to get me what I want, gets the commission."* What are the odds? Not too high. And the truth of the matter is, when a great property does come on the market and the priority buyer conflicts with the non-priority buyer, guess who's going to get the first look at the hot new listing? Exactly...

This is the mentality that you want to instill in the buyer during your presentation. Because otherwise, it's too easy for them to assume that you will call them immediately if something great comes up. Not likely!

Let your potential client know how it really works. Tell them that you and/ or your partner have multiple clients right now who've signed this brokerage agreement – that will make them the fifth one. If you're usually limited to 4-7 clients, then they will know that they are a priority and the buyer brokerage is the way to ensure this level of attention, respect and precedence.

Buyers without Contracts

Naturally, the invention of a buyer broker agreement doesn't stop buyers from asking for a free pass. We get calls all the time from buyers who simply won't sign a contract. But they will still expect your service – you will need to call around and look for properties for them, as well as look for the For Sale by Owner properties coming onto the market, and the expired listings, too…

This is why you must be committed to the contract approach. Any half-assed attempt to receive a buyer brokerage will fail. Guaranteed. If you even suggest that you will consider working with a buyer without them signing this contract, then you've undermined it and sabotaged yourself in the process. Why would they sign it, if they can get you to work without a commitment?

Therefore, it's important that you make this agreement part of your business. There's no half-way on this – you have to commit to it, or else it won't work.

Sometimes it's not the buyers who are the tough sale. From our experience, there are agents who don't get it – they feel no investment with these buyers, so there's nothing to lose, and why sign the contract… However, consider this, would you take a seller's listing tomorrow if they won't sign a contract? No, you wouldn't. The typical response from an agent is, with a seller, they are concerned about the costs for the advertising, the time and energy of listing it, etc. So, why would you give up another buyer to spend your time on an unsigned gamble, taking away time from your family and life, only to not get paid??

This is why the agreement is a crucial tool for getting you and the buyer into a relationship which is most fruitful for both of you.

The Truth is Out There!

When we go through this process of a buyer brokerage, what routinely blows our minds is the truth that comes out of asking these buyers to sign on the dotted line!

It's amazing what is really going on in their minds and this might be the only way to cut to the chase...

Ultimately, it's a perfect opportunity to find out the **Buyer's Intent** – when you think about it, they have nothing to worry about signing, unless they're going to use and abuse you intentionally. If they're not going to do that, then there's really no reason not to sign. Ask them about the buyer brokerage and if they have concerns about signing, you can often get to the bottom of the real situation.

Alan's most experienced agent, arguably the best buyer's agent in San Diego, met with a very nice couple and everything was going swimmingly. He sent them home with a contract to review. But, the next day, he received a phone call from the couple who explained that they we were told by the husband's sister not to sign the documents. Of course, he asked, *"Why?"* The answer was simple, *"Because she's a REALTOR® in Los Angeles and she would like to write up the offer for us when we find our home. Can we still work with you?"* Some of you reading this will be shocked by such a story, and those of you with much experience will simply chuckle in agreement with similar situations. The great news for us is that this agent spent no more than 1 to 2 hours in a meeting in the office before discovering the malicious intentions of these buyers. Seriously... can you believe their sister... another REALTOR® was teaching them how to use and abuse someone in her own industry? The truth is that this scenario is not uncommon in our line of work. Even more frustrating is that we, the industry, are the ones who allow it.

What other business would enter into a relationship without any arrangements for payment? Can you hire a lawyer without paying a retainer? Or go to a doctor without signing anything? A CPA? No. Even a taxi cab driver expects payment when he picks up a fare and drives them all over town.

Without this critical conversation, initiated due to the buyer brokerage agreement, our colleague was about to be used and abused – it's very easy to spend 300 hours assisting a buyer, but this was going to be time down the drain. In effect, the sister, another REALTOR®, was educating this couple in a crash course of 'how to abuse another REALTOR®!

But it's not illegal, it's simply unfair. Now that procuring cause is gone, mostly because it was too difficult to prove, the focus has shifted from the relationship between agents to primarily the relationship between the buyer and the agent. It's all about the representation of the client. So, here we are, with stories like these — time-wasters in clients' clothing. Unless you like opening doors without getting paid, you would be wise to establish the ground rules of the buyer-agent relationship as soon as possible, to avoid misunderstandings like these.

Without having that all important buyer brokerage conversation, we have no one to blame but ourselves.

Promoting the Buyer

Another crucial part of the role of representing the buyer is showing sellers why these are the right buyers for their home.

Let them know in your Buyer Presentation that you're going to tell sellers about them; you're going to understand them and promote them as the best buyer — this is a good family to buy this house. And this can be key when in a hot market or especially in a multiple offer scenario.

Inversely, you will also advise the buyer if this home is <u>not</u> a good deal and <u>not</u> a good fit for their family. For instance, during the inspections stage, if there are problems that become apparent, then you might be obliged to tell the buyer that we need to get out of this deal — or at the very least reduce the offer price in consideration of these new developments. This is why it pays to be represented by a professional who is local and knows the ropes.

This is just one example of the fires that can erupt in escrow. Good luck having a new person handling that, as it can be a nightmare. Which is why we always say, *"You don't count 'em, till you close 'em."*

Showing Homes to Buyers — Tips

1. Bring Your Checkbook

We tell our buyers to bring their checkbook in their back pocket. Basically, they should expect to fall in love — every time they go out with us, they may find the home they want.

This isn't about making a knee-jerk compulsive offer; it is about trusting their instincts and not missing out on a great home, which might not be there tomorrow!

Suggest to your clients that we go out to *buy*, not to look.

2. Don't Rush Them

> Rick says: *"I've seen thousands of buyers walk through model homes that I've sold. What usually works best is when you give those folks some space in the house and tell them that you are giving them space. Some agents walk around with them, joined at the hip, pointing out every little cubbyhole... I prefer to tell them, 'Feel free to walk around and I will catch up with you later and answer any questions.' If the answer is 'no' let them be, but if they're warming up to the house, ask them, 'Can you see how your furniture will fit in the living room?' Once you get the wife hooked, that's who buys the house..."*

In California, we see many wife-wife situations, and husband-husband, too. But, at the end of the day, there's always a "wife."

Ultimately, it's likely the biggest purchase of their lifetime – you can't rush them into an uncomfortable decision, but by educating them, they can make an informed decision quickly that they are comfortable with.

3. Help Them See What They're Looking For

It's always tricky when we know there's something good for them, but they can't see it. It's not a bad idea to carry a clipboard with you, with a check list. *"Did it have the kind of yard you wanted? It has a big kitchen; is this the right size?"* Show them you know what they want and help them see it, in case it didn't register in their minds. It's all about weighing up what they really want.

By creating a list and ticking off all the right boxes, you can review their goals and readjust their perspective if they're on a beer budget with champagne taste.

4. Never Pigeon-hole

While it's smart to show the buyer that you're wired into their criteria for a new home, it can be dangerous to pigeon-hole them too rigidly, as we've seen many u-turns.

> Rick says: *"I've had people that I thought wanted a colonial-style house with a wood-paneled library, and they ended up buying a stark contemporary house. Never pigeon-hole yourself, because if you think you can guess their style, you're wrong. They get to select what houses they see."*

Don't be surprised when a buyer says, *"We want this and that,"* and then fall in love with the complete opposite – it's all emotional. You can't figure it out.

5. Best to Worst?

We've all heard of strategies for showing the worst home first and the best last, so your viewings get increasingly better throughout the day. But, it's a lot simpler to just map the homes and view them in geographical order.

Basically, you want to show them a cross-section of the market. And who knows, maybe they want a fixer-upper?

6. I've Only Seen 3 Homes

When a buyer says they've only seen 3 homes, that's a good time to mention that this was the result of a search of 51,006 homes — we sifted through all of them to find the best 3, as related to what they need and want on their wish list.

For example, based on their budget and criteria, there could be 150 homes in their market with 3 or more bedrooms, but this could be quickly whittled down to 12 if they want a certain neighborhood, with a big backyard.

"We've seen 3 and there are 9 more to see. After these, all we're doing is waiting for homes that come on the market. Our best deals are the ones that are already on the market; the ones that are new won't usually be open to an offer which is, say, $25,000 under asking". This explanation can help to open their eyes — *this is it.*

Thus, yes, there are 51,006 properties at this time, but they're not all for them.

Originally, REALTORS® were concerned about the transparency of having all the MLS data open to the public. But, you can shorten down the buyer cycle by using that data to your advantage — they can see it, so they know you're not hiding anything from them; it's all out there. *"We're just waiting for 3 bedrooms in the neighborhood you like, with the schools for the kids, at the price that you want..."*

7. Great Expectations

Sometimes there will be tough choices and a buyer may need to choose between what they want and having a roof over their head.

It's not uncommon for a buyer to want a home which costs over $400,000, yet they only want to pay $350,000. The allure of that next price range can make it difficult for buyers to see the great deals in front of them. So as agents, we almost need to try and set their expectations really low. If you have those conversations ahead of time, then the buyer should be pleasantly surprised with the $350,000 house.

Of course, there are challenges in every market, whether it's fast or slow. You hardly ever hear that it's an even market. Usually it's one or the other, and the seller thinks it's fast but the buyer thinks it's slow. This is why it can be important to talk about their expectations to make sure they're realistic about what's available in their price range.

Conclusion

For a productive and successful buyer-agent relationship, communication is crucial. Equally so, there needs to be more than just an "assumed" exclusivity – get it in writing, for both of your sakes.

Read on... Chapter 10: Specialties

Chapter 10
Specialties

"There is some place where your specialties can shine. Somewhere that difference can be expressed. It's up to you to find it, and you can."

- David Viscott, psychiatrist, author, businessman

The Blueprint for 100 Deals would be incomplete without taking into account the other ways, outside of a straight-up sale, where homes may come onto the market and be part of your 100 deals. Specifically, these are the real estate specialties that may be inherent to your local area, the result of a change in economic climate, or even tailored due to your own unique interests and abilities.

Although you probably won't rely on a specialty to succeed in real estate, there may be occasions when it's important to balance your business with any one or more of these components on the side.

The secret is knowing your own market, inside and out; in particular the changes that are ahead or currently taking place. Then you can take a glance at the mostly economy-driven specialties, which are opportunities that you may take advantage of.

Below are the specialties that we've seen in the business over the last 25 years...

Builders

Homebuilding companies are putting together all the bricks-and-mortar upfront, in the hopes of making a profit when it's time to sell. And of course, these brand new homes need a representative in the marketplace. While this is typically handled in-house by the builders own on-site sales staff – that is until they move out of the sub-division and on to the next project. In which case, many times they call in a local REALTOR® to sell the handful of homes that are left over, and many times, their model homes.

As far as this specialty goes, builders are good to work with, in any market conditions. They are great sellers. They are motivated and <u>need</u> to sell – even if the market is going down, they need to liquidate their property, as they can't sit there and live in it.

Like many of the other specialties, if you decided to focus primarily on builders and selling new constructions, then you could be suffering in some of the economic times we've been through in the past few years – even if you worked with the biggest building company in the country. Something to bear in mind...

Ultimately, these types of builder listings could be a part of your big plan. It would likely be smaller custom home builders who you would connect with, or builders moving on that will let a local REALTOR® handle their remaining inventory to liquidate their last properties.

Builders need loans to get their work done, naturally. This arena can be difficult during a tough economy, but if you stick around, it will (eventually) come back. Nevertheless, when markets go down like this, the land values go down too, so new home prices come closer to the similarly located resale prices, narrowing the gap between the two.

We would say that there's always a market for new home sales, because when a buyer looks at a resale home versus a new home – if those costs are aligned – there are always people who want brand new. It's just like when they want a new car over a used car; the same is true with a house – especially one that can be customized, so they can make selections on upgrades, features and finishes.

Short Sales

This is another way of saying "pre-foreclosures." Essentially, we're contracting with the current owner of the property and helping them to find a buyer, as well as negotiating down the amount of the loan they owe on the home with the current bank.

As a 'short sale' owes more on their home than what the current market value will net them, if negotiated properly, the bank should discount the note on the home to somewhere consistent with current market values, and even pay for a seller's closing costs, commissions, etc. Why do they do this? Well, the banks do this with an understanding that this process is less expensive for them than the cost of simply waiting for the seller to just let the home slide down the slippery slope into foreclosure.

There are many different nuances to short sales, which you will need to be aware of, should you take this route. However, if short sales are a big part of the market in your area, then you may decide that it's worth becoming an expert in this niche.

As we've mentioned, to get to 100 deals, it's all about knowing what is selling in your market. Should you find that 50% of the sales in your neighborhoods are short sales, then you need to know what's selling, how to do it, and adjust your business accordingly.

Foreclosures

We saw this situation with mortgages during the RTC crisis in the mid to late 80s, and we're seeing this again today. This is a specialty which necessitates building some cordial ties with the banks that you will be working with, in order to get these foreclosure listings directly from them.

Asset managers are your contacts at the banks and to get them on your side, we created a tool called ForeclosureFeedback in the same vein as HomeFeedback, except ForeclosureFeedback facilitates this relationship with Asset Managers and shows them you have the necessary tools that make you an expert in handling foreclosures.

Of course, the listing presentation needs to be geared towards representing these banks, which are not as bought in emotionally as home sellers; instead it's all business and numbers. Be ready to show them how you can help over an agent not as well versed in this area.

By giving the Asset Manager that ongoing transparency to view all of the bank's listings with you, all on one page, they can be impressed and reassured knowing they will be able to see how many showings are taking place, the feedback of agents, and other comments that tell them specifics they might not be aware of (e.g. the plumbing is ripped out, but they wouldn't know, as perhaps they've never set foot inside the foreclosed property). They can also document price changes from the feedback statistical reports and add this to their files.

In order to get these foreclosure listings, it's imperative that you establish these relationships with the Asset Managers at the bank; otherwise, you won't even have your foot in the door. Unlike a builder, the banks don't have their own sales team, thus they need individual agents, too. Yet, it can be frustrating, especially if you kiss an Asset Manager's ass for ten years, then when you hit that inevitable bump in the road they can leave you high and dry, and all your hard work can be flushed down the drain!

This is a very difficult part of the business to control. As a result, if your business is built 100% around foreclosures, you may find that the funds can be switched off immediately if you lose that relationship. Which is why we wouldn't recommend that you rely on it; truthfully, you can't build a real business around it, as you never know how many foreclosures you're actually going to get. Foreclosures would be a COMPONENT of your business, not the whole enchilada.

Once you have an Asset Manager in your corner, they will handle all communication between the bank and you, as their REALTOR® representation. For each home listing, a BPO (Broker's Price Opinion) will be filled out, which they compare to data they have of the market value of the home. The home is then inspected for condition and a value is determined based on these findings.

Sometimes the home is priced at market value or a few percent above, then this comes down every 3 days; others go 5-10% above market value and slowly creep down.

But, we counsel you, be careful not to dive in headfirst – remember you need to be a specialist in foreclosures!

Potential pitfalls might be: paying to get utilities up and running (many foreclosures are cut-off from their electricity, for instance), and having to front money for repairs, which the banks will, eventually, reimburse to you. It helps if you're good at your book-keeping, as you will often need to keep records and wait for reimbursement.

Foreclosure is a different beast in this industry. Whereas short sales are much more controlled, in comparison; you're still marketing to the public, so it makes better sense as a piece of your overall real estate business. Moreover, in the foreclosure sector, pricing can be critical – you can't under-price, as the bank won't accept it, and you can't over-price, as no buyer will ever buy it. This is why you really need to know what you're doing, how to package the sell, how to walk that pricing tight-rope, and stay in constant contact with the bank, usually on a daily basis.

There's a lot of labor involved – from extensive negotiating, to the banks testing you, and testing the seller for hidden assets, so the seller fills out asset sheets and submits hardship letters.

At the end of the day, due to the time-consuming and highly specialized nature of foreclosures, it might be a better situation if you decide to hire a third party negotiation company or an attorney to do the negotiations.

Auctions
The opportunity may arise to run an auction on behalf of the bank, but more than likely they will auction a home through the county courthouse when it's a foreclosure. You may also be asked to represent a builder of several properties, who needs you to auction properties on their behalf.

This is very specialized area of expertise and there are many auction businesses that work primarily in this field... In our books, we would stay away from auctions if you're going to count on it.

Investment Properties
There are high-end clientele who are always on the lookout for prime real estate opportunities as a sound investment for their money. Usually, you would refer them to someone who handles this, or perhaps you could be that person, if this was your specialty.

The property in question could be a 2-4 bedroom home, a duplex, an apartment building, multi-family units, or commercial units and shopping centers. There's a wide range of avenues for an investor.

It's best for you, and your clients, if you focus on specializing either in commercial or residential properties – one is about numbers, one's about heart. What are you better suited for? Some agents hate to represent commercial real estate, others prefer it.

Alternatively, you could just opt to refer people who are seeking investment properties. FYI – you can typically expect to receive a referral fee in the range of 20-35% commission, although you should get this in writing from the agent you refer them to.

Loan Officers
There are real estate agents who offer loans also, but it's not likely they could simultaneously shoot for 100 deals per year. In the past, if you had your own smaller brokerage company, it wasn't uncommon to have a mortgage division as

well, but times have changed. There's not as much money in mortgages anymore as restrictions have tightened

Escrow

Perhaps you have an affiliation with an escrow company, or maybe you've considering owning an escrow firm on the side. We recommend partnering with an escrow company you're comfortable with, rather than taking up this specialty.

Basically, having an escrow partner can greatly improve how things run and can mean a smoother, easier life for you in your real estate business, as it can get you to the front of the pile quicker, without the headache of juggling two companies at once.

While it's possible to run an escrow company, or even be a loan officer AND a real estate agent at the same time, it's truly a distraction from your ultimate goal. Don't get sidetracked trying to do both – you won't ever reach 100 deals.

Specialty vs. Focus

Specializing can add many excellent strings to your bow, guaranteeing flexibility and diversity in your business that will support you in a variety of economic situations and allow you to seize a wide range of opportunities. Yet, when reviewing the variety of specialties that exist, perhaps one will be a natural fit that will 'find' you, or you can pick and choose what you want to be the best at, versus striving to be the best at all of them. Otherwise, you run the risk of ending up as a Jack-of-all-trades, but master-of-none.

Still, it's important to be aware of the specialist roles you can play, especially if they're a big part of your marketplace and you can't ignore them.

Do's and Don'ts
- *Don't get sidetracked*
- *Do take a look in your marketplace for opportunities*
- *Do move with the economic cycle*
- *Don't specialize at everything, but excel at nothing*

As with all of these specialties, in order to be successful in these arenas, one needs to ideally anticipate it; if it's already happening at this point, you're probably too far behind the opportunity to make it worth the investment.

This won't always be the case, but if you know the market is going to go down, you need to anticipate where the next opportunity will be, as well as when it is heading up.

Being a REALTOR® is all about representing buyers and sellers, and that means being able to assist them in finding as many markets, sectors and niches as possible, where homes and properties are available to buy or sell. But it won't be possible to serve everyone – sometimes the seller is on the brink of foreclosure, sometimes the buyer wants a new home – and you shouldn't worry about mastering any or every specialist role. Though, if you are prepared for the potential opportunities that may present in the years ahead, you can keep your plan on track to succeed at achieving 100 deals per annum!

 KEY 100

Keys to be on your way to 100 deals and over $1,000,000 in commissions

1. **Kryptonite:** You can think you are Superman when you do 20 deals a year, but ego could be your Kryptonite to reaching 100 deals if it is not kept in check.

2. **Systems:** You need a system that works, whatever the condition of the economy; it's imperative to your long term success.

3. **Adapting to the Market:** Knowing your market may mean knowing that advertising in the local paper is a great bang for your buck, but in another market you could be burning hundred-dollar bills and need a different marketing avenue. Focus your business to meet the needs of your specific market. That may mean switching from representing a majority of buyers to representing 'short sale' sellers; it's always pretty obvious where the business is, and you need to adapt accordingly.

4. **There are Always Opportunities:** No matter the economy, some people buy. Of course, many consumers pull in their belts during uncertain economic times, although there are those who aren't impacted negatively by these downturns. While some people cut coupons, others buy mansions. Are they buying from you? That's the real question you need to be asking yourself.

5. **Stagnate or Grow:** In the words of Winston Churchill, *"Attitude is a little thing that makes a big difference."* This is an ongoing tide of change, as we can never be 100% certain of market conditions, which is precisely why we need a system that isn't reliant on any particular economic landscape. Thus, throughout the

economic highs and lows of tomorrow, there are ultimately only two options: Stagnate or Grow.

6. **Attract New Clients:** For your practice to work, you must attract clients and provide value. Once again, this is true in any economy, up or down, you need to consistently grow your business and make it as successful as possible, in order to survive – and thrive!

7. **Align with Tech:** You don't need to be a "Techie" to use technology. If you are not comfortable using technology and are more of a face time person than a Facebook person, this does not have to be a barrier for you to provide tech for your clients that require it. Know this is a blind spot of yours and seek help. Align yourself with a brokerage that is tech savvy, has automated systems in place and does this for you, or perhaps your first hire is a tech savvy team administrator or intern to help you. Others can do all of this for you and you can list and sell homes.

8. **Top 5 Benefits of Technology:**
    - *Streamlining – having systems in place and automating tasks*
    - *Real Time – access real time data for solutions*
    - *Flexibility – be able to change with speed*
    - *High Profile – branding, high visibility*
    - *Transparency – websites and software offer transparency*

9. **Media Advertising:** Do not invest in these media unless you are already receiving positive cash flow from them.

10. **Forward Thinking:** We must align ourselves with good brokerage and technology companies that are similarly forward-thinking and let them do the work for us. We must apply an open-minded direction to ensure that we're current and ever-changing with the conditions and temperament of the marketplace. As a result, we can remain even keeled in any economy.

11. **Deal Growing:** After you reach 50 deals in your past 12 months, set yourself a salary that you can pay your current staff, office, marketing, and living expenses and not a dollar more. For the following 12 months reinvest all of your profits back into your business. What to spend those monies on will be addressed later, but here is a quick breakdown of what you need to spend your excess NOI (Net Operating Income) on:

- *Fill your needed staff with the quality personnel you need.*
- *Marketing – websites, SEO, mobile exposure, PPC, social, print.*
- *Smart technology – web based "cloud" software to build and manage your business.*
- *Enhance client services – unique services you offer, transparency solutions to build trust.*
- *Image improvement – office location, office furniture and signage, presentation room, logo upgrade.*

12. _Do_ Go for 100; _Don't_ Stretch Your Limits...

13. **Your Number of Deals:** It may take some time to figure out the perfect number for your team, as every real estate business is different. Though, as a rough guideline, the size of a team for 100 deals is a minimum of 6 to 7 key players – this would probably be 4 sales people (including the leader) and 3 administrative personnel.

14. **Emporing Technology:** *"The number one benefit of information technology is that it empowers people to do what they want to do. It lets people be creative. It lets people be productive... It is all about potential."* – **Steve Ballmer, CEO, Microsoft**

15. **Tech Savings:** Consider the cost benefits, for instance. Did you know that, when using automated technology properly, you can save the full annual salary of a staff member!

16. **Critical Team:** In building our Blueprint for 100 Deals, the Team is undoubtedly the most critical architecture to put into place. Each team member will play their role as a vital cog in the machinery of your real estate business. The administrational members of your team will act as the backbone, and the sales agents will be the life blood, which – when working together as a strong cohesive unit – will take you and your 'Dream Team' to the top.

17. **Be or Join a Team:** In the words of Tom Ferry, renowned real estate **coach** and speaker: *"Either be the team leader... or join a team... it's the future of our industry."*

18. **Team Players:** There are numerous players on a team. Whether you are planning who you might need onboard, or you're assessing what part you will play on an existing team, there are the key personnel that are essential for a successful real estate business.

19. **Tech Team:** Think of technology as part of your team. Technology is cheap compared to personnel. You need to have systems that will replace mundane tasks and save time for team members.

20. **Alan's Team Players Recipe for 100+ Deals Success:**
    Team Players:
    1 Team Manager
    4 Buyers Agents (at a minimum)
    3 Admin Assistants

21. **Alleviate Burnout:** While it's possible there are exceptions to this rule of working in a twosome, the focus needs to be reaching 100 to maximize your efforts, instead of burning out and languishing at 50 deals or less. This ultimately means seeking a team with a number greater than two.

22. **Productive Teams:** *"Highly productive people are attracted to highly productive offices."* - **Carol Johnson, President of The Recruiting Network Inc.**

23. **Invest in Your Players:** Ultimately, this is all about building a team <u>and</u> a sustainable business. Investing in the players on your team <u>is</u> the secret to success.

24. **Communication:** Without good communication, you don't have a business. Whether you're staying in touch via telephone, face-to-face, IM, text or email, communication is the interpersonal 'glue' that holds everything together – cementing the foundations of your team, and sealing every crack to create a seamless and cohesive unit.

25. **Effective Marketing Tools:** When asked to rate the effectiveness of marketing tools, using a sliding scale, real estate agents concluded the following, with 1 = extremely ineffective and 5 = extremely effective:

    - *Word of Mouth (referrals): 4.52*
    - *Personal Sales: 4.05*
    - *Email: 3.72*
    - *Direct Mail: 2.89*
    - *Signage: 2.33*
    - *Telemarketing: 2.04*

26. **Communication Type?** Communication in real estate needs to be often, it needs to be flexible to accommodate the client's lifestyle and characteristics, and it needs to be efficient.

27. **Client Communication:** Success Requires Transparency. Communication with clients today hinges largely on the transparency that you provide them. This transparency is basically giving clients the ability to see what's actually going on with the purchase or sale of their home.

28. **Top Three Seller Complaints:**

   - *The agent doesn't return phone calls.*
   - *The agent doesn't call unless we call first.*
   - *We don't know what the agent is doing to sell our property.*

29. **Frequency of Communication:** How often is often? And how often isn't often enough? See Alan Shafran's frequency grading system to make certain that you're communicating in an effective and time-conscious manner.

30. **Technology CRM (Customer Relationship Management):** All contact information including grading and communication should be kept in a shared CRM (Customer Relationship Management) cloud based software and updated after every contact. Here, all team members can share contacts and the system is available inside the office, form the agents home computers, and via their mobile devices. ShowingSuite.com is an example of this service with their team version for contact and listing sharing.

31. **Stay on Script:** Sales scripts are a huge part of the communication that occurs in the real estate biz. These are tried and tested dialogues that lead to completed transactions. The right script, said the right way, is key to the sales side of the business. Agents on your team need to know these scripts and rigidly follow them; you can't just say whatever you want, any way you want. The training and context is critical.

32. **Capture Leads and Nurture Them:** Communication isn't just about how you conduct yourself with current contacts; it's also about nurturing new leads.

33. **Building a Brand:** Who are *you?* You want the prospects that you capture, and target, to remember your name. The goal of branding is to make your practice or agency synonymous with the best in real estate services.

34. **Client Contacts:** Real estate professionals need to touch their market at least 18 times per year to forge a solid memory, so people opt to call you when they are ready to buy or sell. This means constant communication with them.

35. **Home Feedback:** This is one of the main points of interaction between you and a coop agent, and eventually the client. It can be a bone of contention, and sellers will expect feedback no matter what, so it's very important.

36. **Client Satisfaction:** The final part of the communication process is surveying your clients at the end of a transaction. This provides valuable information about how to improve your business and the communication links between agents and customers.

37. **Social Media:** As long as you're using them in the right way, and efficiently, there are many advantages to blogs, Facebook, Twitter, and other websites for connecting with your consumers.

38. **Testing:** As in fishing, it is not easy to know where the fish are unless you know the waters, conditions and what will make the fish strike at your bait. Unfortunately, there isn't a single answer or specific route to recommend in the practice of fishing. What might work for us, won't necessarily work in a different market with different customers. However, the one thing that does work is testing, testing, and testing.

39. **Fishing for Buyers with IDX:** The main source of buyers can be through a real estate property search website, which involves an Internet Data Exchange, or IDX. Internet users want control with transparency to data and IDX provides this.

40. **Be a Customer:** Many users couldn't differentiate between our sites and *REALTOR.com* – other agents were even framing our free website into theirs. As a result, their clients were actually registering on our site! What is our point? Think like the customer, not like a REALTOR®.

41. **Speed to Lead:** Our recommendation is: where humanly possible – call, email, SMS… whatever. Contact the new leads within an hour. Preferably within 5 minutes. By doing so, assuming that you're presenting yourself properly and professionally, there's no reason why you won't make the first impression – and the best impression – to convert that lead into a client.

42. **Conversion Secrets:** The key is converting as many leads as possible. This means attracting quality leads, and reacting quickly when a new lead arises, but it also helps if you have a solid grasp of who your customers are and the market in your area.

- *Put yourself in the customer's shoes.*
- *Build your website accordingly.*
- *Keep it simple.*
- *Build confidence.*
- *Be reachable, personable, and prompt.*
- *Show value and express quickly why the consumer should contact you NOW!*
- *Close for an appointment.*

43. **Email Automation:** It helps if you use a real estate specific email campaign manager like www.HomeFollowup.com that can integrate with your website. This way, your campaigns start immediately after the prospect signs up from the form on your website and you don't have to copy and paste emailed data.

44. **The Ratio of Leads to Conversions:** With all your nets set, and emails sent, you're probably wondering how many leads it will take to reach a goal of 100 deals...

45. **Marketing Organically:** It's crucial to examine the 'organic' methods of marketing on the internet – these are the unpaid results derived from blogs and raising your profile on 'free' social marketing sites like Facebook. Moreover, through search engine optimization (SEO), the text on your sites and the way your site is optimized can generate more traffic without you paying a cent.

46. **Paid Search:** aka PPC (pay per click). This is what makes Google the multi-billion-dollar juggernaut it is today. PPC are the paid advertisements when you perform a keyword search on a search engine. These ads are typically on the top of the page along with the right hand column. It is a great way to get immediate traffic to your website, but you have to pay for it.

47. **Lead Conversion:** All of this is pointless, even if you're reeling in 1000 leads from your IDX website, if you don't open up a door for these people; you won't succeed in your efforts. Over 80% of REALTORS® don't contact a new prospect in the first 24 hours... This is a huge opportunity for YOU.

48. **Systems You Need to Have in Place:** From the top down, there are several basic systems that every office needs to function at any competent level. These include having the latest computer equipment/hardware and software, to having mobile devices for your team – this is the essential infrastructure.

49. **Tweak the Systems:** You've got to tweak the systems to stay on track. This is simple to do, as accountability and transparency are relatively straightforward when there's a system in place. With a system such as ShowingSuite.com, you can actually see which agent has been given the lead, how they're categorized, who is handling how many escrows, etc.

50. **Apply Systems:** Every aspect of your business needs a system applied to it. This business is all about one deal at a time and it's also about maintaining the system to keep a constant flow and ensure communication and analysis. Unfortunately in real estate, even when you're doing 100 deals a year for 20 years, the real estate industry will punish you if you take your foot off the pedal for a second. It's possible to go from 100 deals to 10 deals in no time at all, just because a couple of your systems are no longer working efficiently.

51. **Save a Tree:** One of the most dramatic, and critical, changes in your Office Systems may be the decision to go "paperless." This will save you dollars, and save the environment in the long-run, but it's a big step and – just like every other system – it needs to have a step-by-step checklist put into place to manage the transition and new process efficiently.

52. **Negotiate:** If you are going to make it to 100 deals, you must master the art of negotiating for all of these parties to feel that they succeeded in the negotiation and resulting transaction.

53. **Value Building:** Ultimately, without demonstrating the added value, you shouldn't be paid more – and you wouldn't pay more if the tables were reversed. YOU WILL NOT WIN LISTINGS IF YOU CAN'T SHOW TREMENDOUS VALUE.

54. **Pick a Side:** Be ready and pick your side before you go into a negotiation. Are you up against a rival, a smaller agent, or a larger agent? Either way, if the clients aren't telling you 'yes' at the end of the presentation, then these factors came up in their minds, but you didn't overcome them.

55. **Highlight and Differentiate:** That's the secret to negotiating and getting the client. For example, discount brokers are notorious for their horrible communication – they'll sign you up and you won't hear from them again. Highlight how you will be communicating with the client on a regular basis. Show them the transparency that they will have during the listing, as well; they may be impressed to learn about how you will communicate information

to them, such as, *"I'm going to provide a seller web portal so you can see all the activity that happens on your house – this is how it's going to be different."*

56. **Discount Brokers:** On every Listing Presentation, you have to overcome any of their doubts that going with a full-service commission is the best decision they'll ever make. Consequently, if you truly want to be 100% sure that you will succeed in a negotiation of commission versus a discount broker, you should get the tools that you need to win these deals and deliver the results the sellers are looking for.

57. **Objections:** Following the Listing Presentation, if the decision isn't going in your favor and the potential client says 'No', you must not be afraid to ask them why they don't want to list with you. For instance, is it because of the commission?

58. **Listing Paperwork:** Of course, until the ink is dry on the paperwork, no listing is secure. As a seller might interview as many as five agents (or more) before settling on the actual agent to sell their house, it's important to get the paperwork filled out, preferably after the Listing Presentation and in person to officially close the listing deal.

59. **Motivation:** It's crucial to know: what are the buyer and seller's motivation? This will drive the entire deal.

60. **Buyer Brokerage:** Our industry has changed in recent years as we now sign buyer brokerage agreements, in the same way sellers sign listing agreements. This has dramatically evolved the way we negotiate with the seller and negotiate with the buyer.

61. **Exclusive Buyer Brokerage:** Buyer brokerage agreements are critical, and we won't enter negotiations without one. Yet, to sign a buyer, once again you must negotiate and share the value of signing that agreement – let them know, *"We're going to spend the time now working for you, so we need to be exclusively representing you."* Have a brief buyer presentation to show them, similar to your listing presentation, and at the close, ask for the signature on the buyer brokerage agreement.

62. **Amount to Negotiate:** When appropriate, it can be healthy to negotiate a little bit – even if you're not far off an ideal price and terms. You can ask about closing a week earlier, or that they use your escrow company, or even request

another $500 off the price... But, remember, this isn't about jeopardizing the deal, it's about <u>solidifying</u> it!

63. **Negotiate for Your Client:** First and foremost, always negotiate for your client, and not for your own profit. And always put ego in the back pocket, otherwise you could eliminate the possibility of this deal working out. Finally, remember to do everything you can to make everybody feel good about what's happening. If you are doing 100 deals a year the chances are you are going to work with this client and this agent again.

64. **Multiple Offers:** Generating multiple offers is possible, whether you're in a fast or slow market... HomeFeedback.com can show you how – in a fast market, we can let every agent who has shown this property know that we have an offer coming in, with a deadline to make a decision by Friday. We would automatically send an email to every agent who showed this home to their clients and advise them, *"Now would be a great time to make an offer."*

65. **Listing Motivation:** *"Why list today?"* This is a big question at the end of every listing presentation. Time is of the essence, but the decision to list will depend on one factor alone – the Seller's Motivation is always more important than the Agent's Motivation.

66. **Timing for Selling:** The message that we convey to sellers is that there is always the possibility that you could lose money on your home when you wait. Your home is not a liquid asset; you can't press a button and make your money back.

67. **Listing Presenter Order:** In a best case scenario, you want to be the first agent through the door. Some REALTORS® strive to be the last one, in order to stand out from their competition that was sitting in the same chair before them, to benefit from the seller's learning curve. However, if you're not the first, you might not ever get the chance to be last...

68. **Partner with Better Known Agents:** There are many advantages to being on a team, especially when you can go into a listing presentation and sell your partnership, or even name your team leader as the co-lister. Let them know that your team has had many sales, does a lot of advertising in the area, etc, and then you can benefit from these assets.

69. **Big Zero:** <u>Alan says:</u> *"Don't ever forget about first place. Before every listing presentation, I would write a big zero on a piece of paper, then draw an anti-sign across it. This reminded me that if I didn't take that listing now, I had zero percent chance of the homeowners calling me back later — It's all or nothing."*

70. **Buyer Expectations:** The buyer broker contract now has a clear-cut template. Ensure that both buyer and agent are on the same page regarding each other's expectations.

71. **Your Buyer Message:** Ultimately, the Buyer Presentation needs to state explicitly, *"I'm going to find the best home for your needs, I'm going to negotiate the lowest price, I'm going to secure the best financing, and finally meet your home-buying needs with the least amount of hassle."*

72. **Buyer Contract Approach:** You must be committed to the contract approach. Any half-assed attempt to receive a buyer brokerage will fail. Guaranteed. If you even suggest that you will consider working with a buyer without them signing this contract, then you've undermined it and sabotaged yourself in the process. Why would they sign it, if they can get you to work without a commitment?

73. **The Best Buyer:** Let the buyer know in your Buyer Presentation that you're going to tell sellers about them; you're going to understand them and promote them as the best buyer — this is a good family to buy this house. And this can be key when in a hot market or especially in a multiple offer scenario.

74. **Bring Your Checkbook:** Tell buyers to bring their checkbook in their back pocket. Basically, they should expect to fall in love — every time they go out with us, they may find the home they want.

75. **Specialties:** Although you probably won't rely on a specialty to succeed in real estate, there may be occasions when it's important to balance your business with any one or more of these components on the side.

76. **Anticipation:** As with all market specialties, in order to be successful in these arenas, one needs to ideally anticipate it; if it's already happening at this point, you're probably too far behind the opportunity to make it worth the investment.

Key 100 Technologies

Technologies we recommended using for 100+ deals, year after year. To receive a current list and updates to technologies we find and like for our business and yours, go to www.blueprintfor100deals.com/tech.

Productivity
HomeFeedback.com
HomeFollowup.com
ShowingSuite.com
Sendoutcards.com
Google docs
Google apps
Docusign

IDX
Realestatewebmasters.com
Diversesolutions
Realtysoft

Listing Syndication
Listhub.com

Social
Facebook
Twitter
Activerain

Real Estate
Zillow.com
Trulia.com
Realtor.com
Redfin.com
Ziprealty.com

Real Estate News
RISmedia.com
Inman.com

Business Analysis & SEO
Google analytics
Hubspot.com

Mobile
Droid – Xoom
iPhone – iPad
ShowingSuite

Electronic Lockboxes
Sentrilock